STRANGE BUT TRUE TALES

SPOOKY KIDS

Bruce Nash and Allan Zullo

Rainbow Bridge®

Troll Associates

LIBRARY OF CONGRESS CATALOGING-IN-PUBLICATION DATA
Nash, Bruce M.
    Spooky kids: strange but true tales / Bruce Nash and Allan Zullo.
        p.   cm.
    ISBN 0-8167-3447-X (pbk.)
    1. Children—Psychic ability—Case studies—Juvenile literature.
[1. Psychical research.   2. Extrasensory perception.]   I. Zullo,
Allan.   II. Title.
BF1045.C45N37   1994
133.8—dc20   93-44029

Cover photograph by Steve Dolce.
Special effects by Shi Chen.

*To Rick Rosen, for his encouragement and,
most importantly, for his friendship.*
Bruce Nash

*To Allison Manausa's third-grade class, who, if they look into
the future, will see they can reach whatever goals they have set
for themselves.*
Allan Zullo

CONTENTS

STRANGER THAN FICTION

You are about to enter the strange world of the unexplained — a world where eerie things happen that defy explanation.

Some kids claim they have the bizarre powers to read another person's mind, predict the future, send and receive messages by thought alone, see the invisible, or pick up psychic vibrations from everyday objects. Some insist they have floated outside their body or have lived in a past life.

This book contains ten spooky stories based, in part, on cases taken from the files of noted experts who investigate strange happenings that cannot be explained by science. The names and places have been changed to protect everyone's privacy.

Could these weird experiences happen to you? Only if you are psychic!

THE FINE LINE

Snuggled on the couch, sixteen-year-old Lisa Fine was watching Janet Jackson's latest video on MTV when she experienced the most bizarre sensation of her life.

As she watched Janet sing "Where Are You Now," Lisa began hearing an entirely different song — "Can't Help Falling in Love" by the group UB40.

What's going on here? Lisa wondered. *Is there something wrong with the station? Do they have their signals crossed?*

But then she realized the tune wasn't coming from the TV. It seemed to be coming from her head!

While she gazed at the TV, the perplexed teen began seeing flashes of a disturbing scene in her mind. It was like an out-of-focus videotape of a car skidding out of control, crashing into a tree, and then flipping over into a ditch. Three times the scene appeared in front of her eyes for only a few seconds, and then disappeared as her eyes once again focused on the Janet Jackson video. But through the flashes, Lisa kept hearing the same UB40 song.

Before the startled teenager had a chance to figure out what was happening, her head and neck started throbbing in pain and her left arm hurt even worse. Suddenly, it all became clear to her. She leaped off the couch and in a frantic voice shouted, "Oh, my God! Laura's been hurt!"

* * *

Like many other identical twins, Lisa and her sister Laura were very close. They thought alike, dressed alike, and laughed alike. They wore their long, blond hair in a French braid that each would twist for the other every morning before school. They applied the same makeup to accent their creamy skin and dazzling sky-blue eyes. Tall and gangly but extremely athletic, they both starred on the high school basketball and track teams.

In their freshman year, Lisa ran for class president and Laura for vice president. They won. The next year, Laura ran for president and Lisa for vice president. And they won again.

The girls enjoyed doing things together, like working part-time at a yogurt shop. Hardly a week passed without neighbors seeing the Fine twins in-line skating in the summer in the park and ice-skating in the winter on the pond a few blocks from their house in Milwaukee, Wisconsin.

The girls were always going to movies and dances, or hanging out with their friends. Lisa and Laura looked so much alike that they would sometimes trade places and pull jokes on their friends by pretending to be each other. Half the time, their friends had no idea whether they were talking to Lisa or Laura.

From the time they were toddlers, the Fine twins displayed a remarkable bond between them — a bond they later began calling the "Fine Line."

Once, when they were four years old and playing in the park, Lisa was on the teeter-totter with her older brother Larry when she fell off and skinned her knee. At that exact moment, a few hundred yards away and out of view, Laura was walking with her mother when she cried out, "Ouch, my knee hurts me, Mommy."

Another time, when they were eight years old and on vacation with their family at Walt Disney World, Laura got lost in Tomorrowland. She had told her family she was going to the bathroom, but no one heard her. When they finally realized she wasn't with them, they started a desperate search. Meanwhile, Laura was looking for them. Finally, she stopped at the front of Space Mountain and, concentrating very hard, sent a mental message to Lisa. Two minutes later, Lisa led her family to Laura.

Then there were the dreams. Every year or so, one of the girls would have a nightmare that somehow would be linked with the other twin's dream. Once, when they were ten years old, Laura dreamed she had been grabbed from the school yard by two masked men. They tossed her into a yellow car and drove off to a lighthouse. There, she was bound and gagged by the kidnappers, who were demanding a ransom from her parents.

While Laura was in the midst of the nightmare about her abduction, Lisa was dreaming she looked out her classroom window and saw two masked men throw her sister into a yellow car. Lisa dashed out of school, hopped on her bicycle, and chased after them. But before Lisa's dream continued any further, Laura woke up from her nightmare with a scream that jolted Lisa out of her sleep.

"I had this terrible, terrible nightmare," Laura told her sister. "Two mean men grabbed me..."

"From the school yard?" asked Lisa.

"Yes. And then they threw me in the trunk of a car..."

"Was it a yellow car?"

"Yes. They took me to a lighthouse and..." Laura stopped, eyed her sister, and asked, "Don't tell me you had the same dream, too."

"I would have saved you if you hadn't screamed and woken us both up," Lisa giggled.

The twins' ability to think alike was never more evident than when they played basketball for the Guilford High School girls' team. Without even looking, Laura always knew where her sister was on the court. Time and again — without a word being said between them — Lisa would break for the basket, and Laura would fire a no-look pass right to her for an easy lay-up. "We were communicating through the 'Fine Line,'" the twins would explain.

* * *

On the night neither girl would ever forget, Lisa came home early from a baby-sitting job down the street. Entering through the back door, she rubbed her cheeks, which had turned red from the wintry wind.

"Oh, great, you're just in time," Laura told her. "I'm on the way out to hook up with Kim and Sara and some of the guys over at Stacy's new house. Come on along."

"I'm going to pass," said Lisa, taking off her coat and

gloves. "I'm beat. Those Manning kids were a real challenge tonight. Next time it's your turn with those little monsters. Anything happening here at home?"

"Larry decided not to go out tonight because his cold has gotten worse," Laura replied. "But I think the real reason is our dear older brother got into another argument with Alycia. He's up in his room watching some boxing match. And, oh yeah, Mom called. She and Dad are having a great time in New York, and they'll be flying home Sunday afternoon. So that's the news update from the Fine household. Are you sure you don't want to come with me?"

Lisa shook her head. "It doesn't seem to be worth it. Now that Stacy has moved out to the country, it's going to take a half hour to get to her house. By the time you get there, you'll only be able to spend an hour before you have to get back here by curfew — unless, of course, you plan on ignoring it since Mom and Dad are out of town."

"I'll be back in time. But if I'm a few minutes late, it'll be for a good reason."

Lisa raised her eyebrows and smirked. "That reason wouldn't be a certain classmate named Jason, would it?"

"Well, he *is* awfully cute," said Laura. "And Stacy said he asked her if I was going to be there tonight."

Lisa playfully jabbed her sister in the ribs and jokingly said, "He must have been a little confused. He probably was asking about me."

"In your dreams, girl!" Dangling the keys to one of the two family cars, Laura added, "Last chance for you to come."

"I'm staying in for the night. Have fun... and say 'hi' to Jason for me."

Laura laughed as she closed the storm door and headed

toward the garage. Suddenly, Lisa had a strange feeling in the pit of her stomach — the kind she would get whenever she was really worried. For a reason she couldn't explain, she turned around, opened the door, and shouted, "Hey, Laura!"

"Change your mind?"

"No," Lisa replied. "Just be careful driving tonight, okay? Especially around Sloan's Curve."

"Sloan's Curve? That's on High Crest Road. I don't go anywhere near there to get to Stacy's, you know that."

"You're right," admitted Lisa, wondering herself why she would have even mentioned that dangerous curve. "I don't know what I was thinking."

"Don't worry about me," said Laura. "I'm an experienced driver. I've had my license for a whole six months!"

Lisa went into the kitchen and fixed herself some hot chocolate. Then she popped into Larry's room and asked, "Who's winning the fight?"

"Holyfield," he answered.

"No, I'm talking about you and Alycia."

Larry flung his pillow at Lisa, but she slammed the door before it had a chance to hit her. Clad in her favorite sweat pants and an oversized Green Bay Packers sweat shirt, Lisa went downstairs, plopped on the couch, grabbed *Seventeen* magazine, and turned on MTV.

Every once in a while throughout the rest of the evening, an unexplained wave of concern would sweep over her. Lisa tried to ignore it, but it just wouldn't go away.

It was shortly after midnight, during Janet Jackson's video, when Lisa began seeing in her mind those frightening images of a car crash. The scenes were fuzzy at first, but they soon came into sharper focus: a rainbow painted on a barn door ... a deer dashing out onto a country road ... a white compact car spinning out of control, smashing into a guardrail, skidding across the road, hitting a tree, and flipping over in a ditch. And through it all, Lisa kept hearing UB40's hit "Can't Help Falling in Love."

The bewildered and frightened teen suddenly experienced a terrible pain on her left side. Her arm felt as though it had been broken, and her skull and neck felt like they had been cracked. The pain was getting stronger and stronger, and the song louder and louder. The images became clearer ... until finally Lisa realized what it all meant: Laura was lying hurt inside the family's white Ford Escort overturned in a ditch!

At first, Lisa tried to tell herself it was just her overactive imagination. But she couldn't kid herself. She knew when she was in tune with her sister on the "Fine Line." And this was one of those times!

Maybe this is a warning, she told herself. *Maybe there's still time to stop the accident.* Lisa raced to the phone and called Stacy. As she frantically dialed the number, Lisa pleaded, "Please, Laura, please be there."

"Hello?"

"Stacy? This is Lisa," she said in a trembling voice. "Is Laura there?"

"No, she left about fifteen minutes ago. You sound upset. Is something wrong?"

"I think Laura's had an accident!" Without explaining any further, Lisa hung up. She dashed upstairs and flung open the door to Larry's bedroom. "Larry! Quick! Laura's been in an accident! We've got to find her!"

"What do you mean we've got to *find* her?" asked her startled brother. "If you don't know where she is, how do you know she's been in an accident?"

"I just *know*, that's all! Come on! We've got to hurry!"

As soon as they hopped into their parents' car, Larry asked, "Where are we going?"

"Go out on Spring Creek Road toward Stacy's house."

As they sped off toward the country road, Lisa told Larry about the crash scene that had flashed in her mind. "I'm sure Laura's trying to communicate with me to find her," explained Lisa. Larry had seen enough of the twins' amazing bond to believe Lisa.

But after half an hour of driving on Spring Creek Road all the way to Stacy's house, Larry and Lisa began having doubts. There was no sign of any accident: no skid marks, no busted guardrail, no toppled tree, and no car in the ditch.

"I don't understand," said Lisa. "The images I saw and the pain I felt were so real. This doesn't make sense. I know she's out there somewhere and she's hurt."

"Let's use Stacy's phone," Larry suggested. "We can call home to see if Laura…"

"Sloan's Curve!" shouted Lisa. "That's where Laura is! I'm positive."

"But that's on High Crest Road a couple miles out of the way. Why would she be there?"

"I don't know why. But she's there! Hurry!"

Ten minutes later, they roared past a barn with a rainbow painted over the door.

"Slow down!" Lisa said. "There's the barn I saw. Right up ahead we should find Laura."

A moment later, they came to Sloan's Curve — a dangerous, winding double-S stretch of road that had been the scene of several serious accidents over the years. "There's a busted guardrail!"

"Look!" shouted Larry. "Skid marks!" He slammed on the brakes and turned the car so the headlights could shine on the streaks of rubber on the road. They led to an embankment where a birch tree had been knocked down. Larry and Lisa leaped out of their car. As they peered over the embankment, Lisa gasped. About thirty feet below, out of sight from the road, lay their white Ford Escort upside down.

"It's our car — exactly like I saw it!"

They half-scrambled, half-slid down the side of the snow-dusted ditch to the smashed-up car. Larry climbed through the driver's side window, which had been shattered.

"I've found Laura!" he yelled. "She's unconscious, but she's alive!"

"Don't move her. I've got a feeling there's something seriously wrong with her head and neck. I'll bet her arm is broken too. Come on out, Larry, and go get help. I'll stay here with Laura." Larry crawled out, took off his coat, and handed it to Lisa. "Put this over her. I'll go to the farmhouse we just passed and call for an ambulance."

Lisa squirmed into the car and began to cry when she saw Laura lying like a rag doll on the ceiling of the overturned car. Lisa gently tucked the coat around her injured twin. "Hang in there, Laura, hang in there," she murmured. "Help is coming."

Only then did Lisa realize that the car's tape deck was still playing.

The song sent chills down Lisa's spine. It was UB40's "Can't Help Falling in Love"!

Lisa and Larry paced the emergency-room waiting area for hours. The rays from the morning sun were just peeking through the window when Lisa spotted Dr. Springer walking down the hall.

"Laura's going to be all right," Dr. Springer announced. Lisa collapsed into Larry's arms, and the two of them sobbed with relief. "She has a broken right arm, a concussion, and a fractured neck," the doctor added. "I understand that when you found her, you didn't move her. That was the best thing you could have done for her. How did you know not to move her?"

"I had a feeling, that's all," Lisa answered.

"Had you moved her the wrong way, it could have caused serious damage to her neck," the doctor explained. "She might even have wound up partially paralyzed."

"When can we see her?" asked Larry.

"You can go in for a few minutes," Dr. Springer replied. "She's still a little groggy from the surgery."

When Larry and Lisa walked into the recovery room, they were shocked by the sight of their sister. Her head was bandaged, her eyes were black and blue, her neck was in a brace, and her arm was in a cast.

"Hi, guys," Laura said weakly. "Heck of a way to get out of going to school for awhile, huh?"

"What happened?" asked Larry.

"Well, I was on my way home, and just as I neared Sloan's Curve, a deer ran out in front of the car. I slammed on the brakes and lost control. The car hit the guardrail, skidded across the road, hit a tree, and rolled over in a ditch.

I passed out, and when I woke up I was hanging upside down. Thank goodness I had my seat belt on. I managed to release the belt, and I fell out of my seat. Then I passed out again, and that's all I remember."

"What were you doing on High Crest Road?" asked Lisa. "Stacy lives off of Spring Creek Road."

"I dropped Jason off at his house," Laura replied. "I had to give him a ride home."

"You *had* to?" Lisa asked with a grin. "Laura, you could have been in that ditch for days, and nobody would have found you."

"I knew you'd find me," said Laura. "I used the 'Fine Line.'"

THE
MYSTERY OF
WILLIE BAKER

ho was Willie Baker?

Why had he always lurked deep in Corey Douglas' memory?

And why did Willie keep popping into Corey's mind every time Corey experienced *déjà vu* — the feeling of having done something before when he never really had?

Not until the age of fourteen did Corey finally unravel the mystery in an incredible discovery that confirmed his wildest suspicions.

* * *

Throughout grade school and into junior high, Corey displayed a remarkable talent for drawing. With a pencil and art paper, he'd sketch everything from the clothes and sports equipment piled up in the corner of his bedroom to the fire station down the block.

His sketches usually focused on things he actually saw — except when he let his mind go blank during a boring class. Then he would doodle in his notebook, usually one of two very different scenes. The first scene was the front doorstep of an old, filthy-looking apartment building. The second was a pretty brick house from long ago. And almost every time he'd think, for just a brief moment, about Willie Baker. Whoever he was.

For as long as Corey could remember, Willie had remained a fixture in his memory, like the face or name of some distant relative he hadn't seen since he was a preschooler. He often tried to call up a mental picture of Willie, but the image always remained too fuzzy. Still, he felt a certain familiarity with Willie, even though Corey had never met him before.

Corey found it odd that he would aimlessly draw those two scenes, because he had no recollection of ever having seen either building in real life. But that soon changed during his first trip to New York City while on vacation with his parents and two sisters.

One day he and his dad were walking on Hester Street in the Lower East Side of Manhattan when Corey froze in his tracks. He stared in awe at an ugly four-story-tall brick apartment building stained by years of city grime. It resembled so many others in the area, except this one had a unique front entrance. Above the door was a large semicircular window bordered by gray, square stones. At the top of the window was a big cement griffin — a mythical monster that was part lion, part eagle.

Corey couldn't believe what he was seeing. "Hey, Dad, look!" he exclaimed. "I've drawn this building! It's exactly like the one I've sketched lots of times before. Have I ever been here? Like maybe when I was little?"

"No, Corey, this is your first trip to New York."

"Then I think I'm experiencing *déjà vu*."

As if nudged by some strange force, Corey walked over to the front stairs that led to a basement apartment. "Dad, something is going on here and I don't understand. I'm getting a real bad feeling about this place. Real bad. But don't ask me why."

Corey took a couple of steps down the stairway when he became overwhelmed with an instant hatred for the place. It held bad memories of loneliness, hunger, and pain. But he couldn't have had such memories. He had never been here before. Besides, he came from a loving, caring family and had never felt the things he was feeling now. It didn't make any sense.

"Corey, are you okay?" asked his father. "You look so pale."

"I'm okay," Corey replied, not very convincingly. "Must be the heat and the foul air around here." They walked away in silence until Corey asked, "Have you ever heard of Willie Baker?"

His father thought for a moment and replied, "No, son, can't place the name."

They ambled down to Baxter Street a few blocks away when Corey faded into the strangest daydream of his life. He no longer heard the honking New York traffic, or smelled the exhaust fumes, or noticed all the people walking in front of him. In his mind, all he saw were hundreds of dirty-faced children in ragged knickers and tattered dresses from another era. Some kids were wandering about, some fighting, others were dashing in and out of alleyways. He saw sweaty horses pulling wagons loaded with barrels, and men in caps and overalls lugging carts of fruits and vegetables. He saw more children sleeping in doorways, under stairways, and on discarded packing boxes. And he felt lonely, fearful, and hungry.

Snapping out of his eerie daydream, Corey said, "Dad, let's get out of here, please. I don't feel so well."

* * *

A few months later, Corey's father, an English professor, landed a teaching job at Ball State University. So the family left Kansas and drove to their new house in Muncie, Indiana. As soon as they neared the city limits, Corey felt a warm, comfortable glow — like he was coming home. That was ridiculous, of course, because he had never been to Muncie in his life. Still, the scenery seemed so familiar: the stone gazebo by the duck pond, the bronze statue of the town's founder, the bridge with the limestone pillars.

"Now, let's see," said Professor Douglas as they entered Muncie. "We need to get to Chelsea Avenue. Do we make a left on Jefferson Street or a right?"

"I guess left," said Corey. Then as a joke, he looked at his watch and said, "With my satellite-beaming tracking device hidden in my watch, I see a sharp curve up ahead that leads to a park. Then another turn or two and you'll be there."

"Okay, we'll give it a shot," said his father, going along with the gag.

To everyone's astonishment, the road made a sharp turn and headed to a park! "Are you hiding a map?" his father asked suspiciously.

"No, honest," said a stunned Corey, who was just as surprised as the rest of the family.

"Then how did you do that?"

"I ... I don't know. It just seemed like the way to go."

"Now where, Mr. Navigator?" asked Corey's father.

"Make a right. I have a feeling we'll come to a three-way intersection with a restaurant shaped like a giant dog on the corner."

His sisters burst out laughing. "Yeah, sure," they said.

A minute later, the car arrived at a three-way intersection, just like Corey said. But there was no dog-shaped restaurant on the corner, only a bank, a gas station, and several antique shops.

"So where's your giant dog?" sassed his sister Katey. "Like there really was one."

The following day, after moving into their rented house, Corey explored the neighborhood on his bike. He had a good feeling about this town — like he belonged. No matter where he went, he never felt lost because everything seemed so familiar, even though it was all new to him.

He rode to Elmwood Park, where kids were choosing up sides for a sandlot baseball game. Corey loved baseball and had been an all-star pitcher on his Little League team back in Kansas.

"Hey, do you want to play?" one of the boys shouted to Corey.

"Sure, but I didn't bring my glove."

"That's okay, you can borrow one of ours. Lefty or righty?"

"Doesn't matter," replied Corey. "I can throw with either hand." And then he proved it by pitching three innings left-handed and three right-handed.

Halfway through the game, while waiting to bat, Corey slipped into another brief daydream. He saw shirtless kids in knickers and floppy caps playing baseball in their bare feet. Their gloves looked like oversized mittens, and the bases were empty burlap bags.

On his way home after the game, Corey wondered why he kept thinking about a different era, first in New York and now in Muncie. And why was Willie Baker haunting his mind with more frequency?

Without paying attention to where he was going, Corey had ridden his bike not to his house on Chelsea Avenue, but to a neighborhood several blocks away. As he crossed a bridge that spanned a swift-moving river, he shuddered because he feared water. Despite all his athletic abilities, Corey had never learned to swim. In fact, he never even wanted to learn.

When he reached the corner of Parker and Highview Avenues, his heart started pounding with excitement. The houses looked so familiar. Stately, brick two-story homes — the kind built at the turn of the century. *Is this déjà vu?* he wondered. *Where have I seen these houses before? In a magazine? In a movie? Maybe they were described in a book I had forgotten about. Or maybe ... no, it couldn't be.*

Highview was a two-block-long street that started at the top of a hill at Parker and sloped to Busby Avenue. Corey coasted down Highview, eyeballing each house with a certain degree of recognition. At the second house from the bottom of the hill, he screeched to a halt and stared in amazement.

It was the very same house he had drawn countless times before! An old, red brick, two-story home featuring a stone chimney and a tall veranda with columns made of flat rock.

More astounding was the eerie feeling that he had been *inside* the house, in fact, that he had even *lived* there!

In his mind, he could see the interior. To the left of the entry hall, the dining room; to the right, the living room; the kitchen, with a brick wall and slate floor in the back; the staircase leading up to two bedrooms and a bathroom.

I'm dying to go inside, but I don't dare, he thought. *What would I say? "Pardon me, but I'd like to look inside your house to see if I remember it, even though I've never been here before. And, by the way, does the name Willie Baker mean anything to you?" They'll think I'm a nut case for sure.*

Reluctantly, he left and then pedaled back to his new house, taking a short cut without even wondering how he knew the quickest way home.

* * *

The daydreams, the drawings, the *déjà vu.* They were leading Corey to suspect one mind-boggling explanation — that he was someone named Willie Baker in another life-time! Either that or he was going crazy. But Corey needed more evidence before he could say anything to his parents.

By pure luck, he found some evidence when he went to the city's main library to do research for a school science project. The library had a display of old photographs from the early 1900s to the 1940s for Local History Week. As Corey casually glanced at the display, he was thunderstruck.

He recognized the first three photos without even looking at their captions! There was the old city jail, the First National Bank building, and the Wilkins Hotel. According to the captions, they all had been torn down years ago, but Corey remembered them anyway.

Then his eyes focused on a picture he knew instantly. "Yes!" he shouted out loud and then cringed in embarrassment when everyone in the library stared at him. He was looking at a photo of the Bulldog Cafe — a building shaped like a giant dog! It stood at the intersection known as Three Corners — right where Corey had predicted it was when the Douglas family first arrived in Muncie! According to the caption, the Bulldog Cafe was built in 1920 and was a city landmark until it burned down in 1967. That was ten years before Corey was born, yet he knew it held some special significance to him.

He eagerly looked at the other photos — most of which he recognized — before he stopped in front of one picture that caused his eyes to fill with tears.

It was a photograph of dozens of children — mostly boys in threadbare clothes — getting off at the Muncie train station. Their faces were etched in a jumbled mixture of fear and excitement, emotions that Corey was feeling himself at that very moment.

He read the caption with tingling interest: "Forty-seven poverty-stricken, unwanted children and orphans from the poorest part of New York City arrived by train to start a new life in Muncie in 1908. These waifs were part of a movement by the Children's Aid Society to place thousands of homeless children in foster homes on the farms and in the towns of America's heartland."

Corey still didn't know what all this meant. But with the help of the reference librarian, he read some historical accounts about the Children's Aid Society. Back in the late 1800s, the streets of New York City teemed with thousands of homeless children.

According to one article, "They were ragged young girls who had nowhere to lay their heads, children driven from drunkards' homes, orphans who slept where they could find a box or stairway, boys cast out by stepmothers or stepfathers, children whose answer to the question, 'Where do you live?' was always the same: 'Don't live nowhere.'

"Even when they had families, the children of the poor were under fearful pressure. Crime, drunkenness in epidemic proportions, and unbelievable overcrowding made growing up in New York a hazardous gamble. In some wards of the Lower East Side, several families frequently lived in a single cellar room. One huge barracks — the 'Old Brewery' at the Five Points, where Worth, Baxter, and Park streets intersected — was 'home' to an estimated 1,500 men, women, and children."

That's it! Corey thought. *New York ... the terrible feelings of that apartment building ... the daydream about all those street kids from the turn of the century ... why I felt sick on Baxter Street ... why I remember things about Muncie!*

Corey dashed out of the library, hopped on his bike, and rode back to the brick house on Highview Avenue. He marched up and rang the doorbell. When an elderly woman answered the door, Corey panicked for a moment, wondering what he would say.

"Pardon me, Ma'am, my name is Corey Douglas. I, uh, I was wondering something. I think this house used to belong to a relative of mine from long ago," he fibbed. "But I'm not sure. Does it have a staircase when you first enter and a dining room on the left and a living room on the right and a kitchen in the back with a stone floor and a brick wall?"

"Why, yes it does," replied the woman.

"How old is the house?" asked Corey.

"Well, let's see. I think it was built in 1908."

"Do you have wood floors in the living room and dining room and two bedrooms upstairs?"

"Yes, how did you know? Have you been here before?"

Corey didn't answer her because he was too excited. Now came the big question. And he couldn't wait to hear the answer. "Does the name Willie Baker mean anything to you?"

She thought for a moment. "No, it doesn't ring a bell. Was that your relative's name?"

"Well, sort of," said Corey, disappointed by her answer. He didn't know what to think now. "You wouldn't know who first lived in this house by any chance would you?"

"No, I sure don't. You probably could look that up at the county courthouse."

"Thank you, Ma'am." Corey started to walk away when he turned around and asked, "Do you still have a big plaster flower design on the ceiling in the dining room?"

"Yes, I most certainly do."

* * *

Corey was so excited when he tried to explain to his parents all that had happened that they ordered him to slow down because he was talking too fast. When he breathlessly finished his account, he announced, "Mom, Dad, I know you'll think I'm crazy, but is it possible that I was ... that I was Willie Baker in another life?"

Although his parents were open-minded, they still had plenty of doubts. So he showed them the house on Highview and then said, "Some of my drawings are still packed in boxes from the move. Dad, you remember that awful apartment in New York, right? If I can find the sketches I drew last year before our trip to New York and our move to Muncie, and they match the apartment and the house on Highview, will you believe me then?"

"Son, that will certainly help build your case," Professor Douglas replied.

Corey anxiously dug through the boxes in the garage and pulled out last year's notebook. He yelped with glee when he found a detailed drawing of the New York apartment and the Muncie house on Highview.

"Corey, you have a strong case, but I don't know if you have any real proof," said Professor Douglas. "Tell you what. One of my colleagues has been doing some research in hypnotic regression — hypnotizing people so they can relive their previous lives. If you're willing, I could arrange for you to undergo a session."

"All right!" exclaimed Corey. "Let's go for it!"

The following week, Corey went to the office of psychologist Dr. Joel Feldman, who agreed to hypnotize the boy and tape-record the session.

While Corey relaxed on the couch, Dr. Feldman said in a soothing voice, "Relax, Corey, close your eyes and take slow, deep breaths. Now picture yourself walking down an empty, dark hallway. Keep walking ... walking ... now you're coming to a door. When you open the door, you will enter into another time and you will witness your previous life. Now slowly open the door ... walk through it ... and tell me what you see."

"I'm in New York," Corey mumbled under hypnosis. "It's 1908 ... I'm ten years old ... and I'm cold and hungry and alone on the streets."

"Do you know your name?" asked Dr. Feldman.

"Baker, Willie Baker."

"Why are you cold and hungry and alone?"

"I've been thrown out. But that's okay. I would have run away soon. My mom's dead and Dad — he's a longshoreman — beats me when he's drunk. We're very poor. We live in the cellar of a one-room apartment on Hester Street. I'm better off in the streets. I make a nickel a day selling papers for the *World-Telegram*. There are lots of kids worse off than me. I eat out of garbage cans or sometimes steal food off a vegetable cart when no one is looking. I'm always getting beaten up by older boys, fighting over food or a place to sleep. I want to get out of here but I don't know where to go.

"The police catch me snatching a purse, and they take me to a social worker. She tells me about the orphan trains and how lots of kids like me are sent to the Midwest to start a new life with a foster family and a home and hot meals and school. It sounds okay, I guess. Anything's better than the way I live now.

"More than forty of us kids get on a steam locomotive, and we're going to Indiana! It's the biggest thrill of my life. I've never been on a train before. I've never seen the countryside. 'What's that, Mister?' I ask the man who's taking us to Indiana. He tells me, 'Cornstalks.' 'Oh, yes, corn. That's what they use to make mush. Do they have corn fields in Indiana? Oh, look! What are those funny-looking orange things?' He tells me, 'Pumpkins.' 'What are pumpkins?'

"We arrive in Muncie on Sunday. It's a bright, sunny fall day and I'm scared to death. We all get off the train, and everyone is quiet, wondering who's going to pick us. Is it going to be someone mean like my dad? Or someone nice, maybe even rich? Oh, I hope it's someone rich. We wash up and comb our hair, and the man tells us to be polite. Then he takes us to a churchyard, and grown-ups in dress-up clothes come over and ask us questions.

"An older man with a big black mustache and a dark suit looks me over. 'What's your name, son?' he asks. 'Willie Baker, sir.' 'Hello, Willie, my name is Donald Henry Lowry. This is my wife Grace.' She's dressed in pink and smells nice. I answer questions about myself — there's not much to tell.

"Then Mr. Lowry asks, 'Is there anything you'd like to ask about us?' So I say, 'Ma'am, are you a good cook?' They both laugh. They seem nice. She says, 'Would you like to come home with us? We don't have children of our own. We have a brand-new house with an empty bedroom that could be your very own. Do you like dogs? We have three bulldogs you can play with in the yard.'

"I think I've hit the jackpot. A house — not a room in the basement — and my very own bedroom and a yard and dogs and everything. Still, I'm scared. 'For how long can I stay?' I ask. 'Forever, darling,' she says. I'm still scared but I'm happy.

"I've never seen so many nice houses and trees. And the streets are so clean and quiet. Now we come to their house. I can't believe it. It's so grand. Prettier than I ever dreamed. Red brick with a tall veranda and pillars of stone and a huge chimney in the front. I run from room to room. One's nicer than the next. My bedroom is upstairs, and I can look down on a yard of green grass. Sure beats looking up at feet walking by on Hester Street.

"That night I can't sleep. I'm too keyed up. I worry maybe this won't last. So I sneak down into the cellar. I get Mr. Lowry's fishing knife, and I carve my initials in big letters in the cellar wall: W.B. I want to leave my mark."

Under hypnotic regression, Corey told how the Lowrys raised Willie with more love than he could ever have hoped for — and he returned their affection. Willie did well in school, although he had to start two grades behind because he had never gone to school in New York. He became a great baseball player who could fire blazing fastballs with either hand. His baseball, bulldogs, and buddies helped make it the happiest time of his life.

But then World War I broke out. Willie enlisted in 1917 at the age of nineteen and fought in France. He survived the war without being seriously injured. The following year, Donald Lowry died of the flu during the deadly influenza epidemic. After the war, Willie returned to Muncie to take care of Grace. In 1920 Willie built a small restaurant shaped like a bulldog at Three Corners. He called it the Bulldog Cafe.

Tragically, in 1926, at the age of twenty-eight, just a few months before he was to be married, Willie died. He was fishing with a friend in the Buck River, which was running high and fast from a recent storm. When his friend slipped off the bank and into the water, Corey jumped in to save him. But neither knew how to swim, and they both drowned.

When Corey was brought out of hypnosis, he felt such a sense of relief — and amazement. Finally, he had found Willie Baker! Those strange memories and feelings that had been swirling around in Corey's head were really his own from another life! Now he completely understood the significance of the Hester Street apartment and the house on Highview. Now he knew why he could pitch with either arm. And now he knew why he was so deathly afraid of water!

If there was any doubt left, it was washed away by two discoveries Corey's parents made while looking through some old records at the county courthouse. They found a death certificate stating that a Willie Baker, age twenty-eight, died from drowning on August 15, 1926. And they found a deed that showed Donald and Grace Lowry had built a house at 707 Highview in 1908. There was only one more unanswered question Corey wanted resolved. He and his parents went back to the house on Highview and were given permission by the owner to inspect the basement. The cellar walls, which were made of limestone, had been covered by layers of paint over the years. Corey prayed that the paint didn't hide the one telltale sign he so desperately wanted to find. Slowly, carefully, he scanned the walls, studying every little crack.

Finally, after shoving an old file cabinet out of the way, Corey found what he was looking for in a forgotten corner. "There it is!" he cried. "There it is!"

Carved deep into the wall were the letters W.B.

THE COIN READER

When Old Man Crimmins died, everyone believed he had left some money behind. But no one knew where he had stashed it.

However, he left a strange clue to its whereabouts for his new friend, thirteen-year-old Sean Davis. It was a clue to a mystery that could only be solved through Sean's special psychic power.

* * *

Walter Crimmins was the weirdest man Sean had ever met.

According to word around the neighborhood, Crimmins was almost a millionaire from making a killing in the stock market. The squat, white-haired, seventy-year-old was a miser and a recluse. He lived alone in a small, two-story house that hadn't been painted in years. He cut his lawn with a push mower, didn't own a car, and bought his clothes at a second-hand store.

A man of few words, Crimmins never let anyone in his house and never stepped foot in anyone else's. He went out only when he had to shop. Otherwise he stayed inside with the shades drawn. Naturally, the neighborhood kids made up wild stories about him and stayed away from him.

Sean was one of the few kids who had actually spoken to Crimmins because the old man's house was on his paper route. And Sean felt sorry for him.

"All he needs is a friend," the boy told his buddies.

"All he needs is a trip to the mental ward," they said.

"He's just a lonely old guy," said Sean.

"With lots of money hidden inside," they replied.

"Don't be silly," said Sean. "No one who has lots of money would live like he does."

One day, shortly after Sean went to Crimmins' house to collect the monthly subscription fee, the boy realized he had mistakenly included his lucky coin in the change he had given to the recluse.

The coin — a 1913 nickel with a buffalo on one side and an Indian head on the other — had been given to Sean by his father, who had received it from Sean's grandfather. Sean had kept it in his pocket for good luck ever since. Somehow the nickel became mixed up with the other change in his pocket.

The next day, Sean returned to Crimmins' house. The door opened. Before the boy could say a word, the old man said, "You're back because you gave me the wrong coin with the change. Am I right?"

"How did you know?" asked Sean with surprise.

"The coin told me."

"Huh?"

28

Gently fingering the buffalo nickel, Crimmins asked, "Have you ever stopped to think about the life of a typical coin? How many people touched it before you did? All the things it helped buy? Who last used it? What significance, if any, it holds for its owner? Take this coin of yours, for instance. To most people it's just five cents. But to you, it's probably priceless. I assume it's been in your family for years."

"My grandfather —"

Crimmins interrupted him. "Ah, yes, his dad gave it to him on the day he was born in 1913. Then your grandfather gave it to your dad on the day he was born, and your dad gave it to you on the day you were born. Am I right?"

Sean, left speechless because the old man was absolutely correct, simply nodded.

"Well, here's your nickel." Crimmins flipped the coin to him. "Oh, by the way, here's a tip for always having the paper on my doorstep when I wake up." Crimmins then tossed him a quarter.

A quarter, thought Sean. Man, this guy is cheap. Most people on my route give me a five-dollar tip at Christmas time. But a quarter?

Crimmins noticed Sean's look of disappointment. "Learn to read the coin, my boy, learn to read the coin." The old man smiled and closed the door.

What did he mean by "read the coin"? wondered Sean. And how did he know all those things about my nickel? Man, this guy is really weird.

That night in bed, Sean studied the quarter Crimmins had given him. *Read the coin, huh? Well, let's see. It's a 1932 quarter, and the D by the year means it was minted in Denver. George Washington is on one side, with the words "Liberty" and "In God We Trust." The other side has an eagle with the words "Quarter Dollar," "The United States of America," and "E Pluribus Unum," whatever that means. Read the coin?*

As he held it in his hand, he began getting flashes in his mind of a coin collection, of Crimmins studying coins with a magnifying glass. *Hey, maybe this coin is worth something. Wouldn't that be cool?*

The next day, Sean visited a coin store and had the quarter appraised. He learned that 1932 was the first year quarters were minted with the profile of George Washington on one side. That made his quarter valuable. Because it was in excellent condition, it was worth $60!

He was tempted to sell it, but for a reason he himself didn't understand, he kept it. Holding the quarter in the palm of his hand, Sean got another mental picture of the old man: misunderstood, sad, and lonely. He wasn't as cheap as everyone made him out to be. In fact, Sean sensed that Crimmins was an extremely generous person. And he had a feeling the old man wanted to see him again.

* * *

"I was hoping you'd come back," Crimmins told Sean. "Please, come in."

It was the first time Sean had been inside the old man's house. The living room was neat and clean, with furniture that reminded Sean of old "Leave It to Beaver" reruns.

"Mr. Crimmins, about this quarter you gave me. I have a feeling you know a lot about coins."

"Very true, my boy, very true. I'm a numismatist — a fancy word for coin collector."

30

"But the quarter is worth…"

"…between $50 and $60. I know."

"Well, thank you. I really appreciate the tip. I've never had one that big before."

"Sit down, Sean. What I'm about to say may shock you, but don't be alarmed." Sean sat on the couch and Crimmins eagerly pulled up a chair facing the boy. "I believe you have a gift, but you may not know it," Crimmins told him. "Have you ever heard of ESP?"

"Extrasensory perception," Sean replied. "Psychic stuff."

"Exactly. Certain people have the ability to communicate through thoughts and feelings. Others can predict the future or see into the past. Some can tell total strangers about themselves simply by getting a vibration off an object. I have that psychic gift, Sean. And I think you do too — only you don't know it."

Sean began to rise from his seat and said nervously, "I better be going now."

"I know what you're thinking, Sean. You think I'm a crackpot, some old fool who's talking gibberish. And you want to leave without hurting my feelings. Am I right?"

"Well …"

"Sit down for just a minute more. I want to give you something to hold." Crimmins removed a silver chain from around his neck. Attached to it was a beat-up old silver dollar that looked like someone had chiseled a big dent in it. Crimmins handed it to Sean and said, "Okay, close your eyes and tell me what you see in your mind and feel in your heart. Take your time."

Sean did as he was told. Slowly, he started to get a picture in his mind. "I see a soldier in battle, like maybe in

World War II. He's been shot — he's bleeding. He's being held by another soldier, who's trying hard not to cry..."

Sean opened his eyes. "Why, it's you! You're the soldier trying to help him!"

Without saying yes or no, Crimmins gently urged Sean, "Close your eyes and tell me more."

"The dying soldier hands you something. It's the coin. You promise to keep it forever ... and he dies..." Sean's voice trailed off. The vision seemed so real. But he was afraid to believe it, so he tried to brush it off. "People say I have a good imagination."

"It wasn't your imagination, son. This silver dollar was given to me by my best friend, Charley Butler, just before he died in my arms during the Korean War in 1951." Crimmins leaned forward and in an excited voice declared, "You see? You do have the gift!"

Sean was too startled to say anything at first. He dropped the coin and said, "I've got to go now. Bye, Mr. Crimmins." Then he scrambled out of the house and raced home. *Is this man crazy?* Sean wondered. *Is he playing tricks? He could have agreed with anything I said. He must be some old coot trying to have fun at my expense.*

Early the next morning on his paper route, Sean tossed the paper on Crimmins' front step when the porch light went on and the old man stepped outside. "Sean, do you have a second? I want to show you something, and then you can go on your way."

Reluctantly, Sean went inside and followed Crimmins to his study where he pointed to a black-and-white photo hanging on the wall. It showed two soldiers side by side in fatigue pants and T-shirts smiling in a sandbag bunker.

"Have you ever been in this room before or seen this picture?" Crimmins asked.

"No, sir."

"Good. Now take a close look and tell me what you see."

"Why, that's you on the left!"

"Correct. Now do you recognize the soldier on the right?"

Sean's heart skipped a beat. It was the dying soldier he had seen in his mind the day before! He nodded weakly.

"Ah, but there's something else. Look what he's wearing around his neck."

"A silver dollar. Like the one you're wearing."

"Charley wore it when we were shipped to Korea," Crimmins recalled. "A few weeks later, during a battle, he was shot near the heart. But this silver dollar took the brunt of the bullet and saved his life. That's why there's this big dent in it. This silver dollar was his good-luck charm. He swore that nothing bad would happen to him as long as he wore it. He never got so much as a scratch after that for months.

"Then one night, I had to lead a dangerous mission. Charley was ordered to stay back, so he gave me his silver dollar for good luck. My squad was ambushed and several of my men were killed. Fortunately, I wasn't shot. We had just returned to our camp, when a fierce battle erupted. Charley was hit. I took off the silver dollar and put it around his neck. But he told me it was too late, and that I should keep it. Then he died in my arms."

For the first time, Sean began to believe that maybe he did have some special ability that couldn't be explained. He told Crimmins about the time he found a lady's watch near a street gutter. Even though he had never seen it before, he had a feeling the watch belonged to Mrs. Dixon, who lived a couple of blocks away. She had indeed lost it.

Then there was the time Sean was collecting donations of used clothes for the local homeless shelter. As he was carrying two big bundles donated by Mr. and Mrs. Winston — neighbors whom he hardly knew — Sean immediately sensed feelings of hurt, anger, and frustration. He couldn't figure out why. A few weeks later, he learned that the Winstons were getting a divorce.

"What you have is a psychic ability called psychometry," Crimmins explained to Sean. "It means you can learn things about people just by holding an object of theirs in your hand and picking up vibrations, thoughts, or visions. There's a theory that everything that has ever existed from the beginning of time has left an invisible trace of its existence. It's like when you take a photograph. The image remains invisible until the film is developed. In psychometry, a few gifted people use their mind to visualize or 'develop' the invisible traces of the object, revealing things about the person who owns it."

"Is that how you knew about my buffalo nickel?"

Crimmins nodded. "We all have our specialties. I 'read' coins. In other words, I hold coins in my hand and can tell things about the people who owned them. It only works if they keep the coin in their possession for a while. You'd be surprised at what you can learn about people. It's like eavesdropping on them or snooping through their diary without actually doing it.

"Anyway, back to your question. I first suspected you might have the gift when you gave me that buffalo nickel by mistake. I received a very clear vision when I read the coin. I learned its family history, and I also 'saw' things about you.

For instance, you get good grades, love your parents, and you've got eyes for a very cute redhead. Am I right?"

"Hey, that's an invasion of privacy!"

"Perhaps, but you read the coin I gave you and learned something about me. Am I right?"

"I guess. Except I didn't know what I was doing."

"It takes patience and concentration to read objects. It works best when the object you're holding has some special meaning or is owned by someone during an emotional time in his or her life. Here, try this." He handed Sean a gold ring. "What can you tell me about the person who owns it?"

Sean played with the ring in his hands, "Well, I'm pretty sure it's a woman ... very sweet ... big-hearted ... liked to help others. Let's see, uh, she loved..." He looked up at Crimmins. "She loved you ... she was your wife."

Crimmins' eyes grew misty. "She was a saint. When she died in that car crash back in 1960, I pretty much stopped living. I shut out most of the world and spent my time buying and selling coins." He began wheezing and coughing. "Say, I'm rambling on and telling you things you don't want to hear. Now be off with you. I'm tired and don't feel so well."

A few weeks later, Sean noticed the newspapers on Crimmins' porch hadn't been picked up in three days. Since the recluse never went anywhere, Sean became worried and knocked on the door. There was no answer. Sean went from window to window until he found one that wasn't locked. He opened it and crawled inside. "Mr. Crimmins! Mr. Crimmins! Are you in here?"

He heard a moan coming from upstairs and bounded up the steps. He found the old man lying in bed, having difficulty breathing. "Mr. Crimmins! I'll get help!" Sean dialed

911 and then sat down beside the stricken recluse.

"I never got around to writing out a will," Crimmins said in a raspy whisper. "And now it's too late." He opened his feeble, shaky hand and gave Sean the lucky silver dollar. "This is for you. Read the coin. Then you'll know what to do."

Crimmins died the next day.

Sean was too upset to get any psychic impressions from the silver dollar. In fact, he couldn't even look at it for a week. Eventually, though, he tried to read the coin. Every day, he would sit down for a few minutes, place the dollar in the palm of his hand, close his fist, and concentrate.

At first, all he saw were the war scenes of Crimmins and his buddy Charley. But over time, other images began to emerge that formed a brief and fascinating history of Crimmins: A battle-scarred veteran returns home from the war and marries his sweetheart. They are very happy. They buy a house, and he works as a stockbroker. The couple get seriously injured in a terrible car accident, and the wife dies. Crimmins survives but sinks into a deep depression, quits his job, and becomes a recluse whose whole life revolves around his coin collection.

But then Sean "saw" two new things about Crimmins: The old man had given away hundreds of thousands of dollars to charity and had hidden away more money. But where? Sean didn't know, but by reading the coin he felt that the photograph of Crimmins and his wartime buddy Charley held the secret.

* * *

After Crimmins' death, Brent Sanders, his long-lost

nephew and only living relative, claimed ownership of the house and all its possessions — including the old man's coin collection, which was valued at $10,000. But Sanders was convinced that his late uncle had hidden more money in the house. So he went from room to room, searching for the cash. He looked through all the drawers and closets and every nook and cranny, but turned up nothing. Then the frustrated Sanders tore up all the mattresses and even the upholstery of the couch and dining room chairs in a crazed effort to uncover the stash. Yet he still didn't find so much as a dime.

Sanders was ripping up the floor boards in the living room when Sean knocked on the door. "Who are you?" snapped Sanders.

"I'm Sean Davis. I was a friend of Mr. Crimmins."

"He didn't have any friends," Sanders said irritably.

"I was his friend and his paper boy."

"Look, I don't have time for you. I'm busy. What do you want?"

"I was wondering. There's a picture of Mr. Crimmins hanging in the study. Would it be okay if I take it, you know, as something to remember him by?"

"Yeah, go ahead. But make it quick."

Sean walked into the study and gently removed the framed black-and-white photograph. When he returned home, he sat the photo on his lap and attempted to pick up any psychic vibes. In his mind, he kept seeing two coins and tens of thousands of dollars. But this vision felt different from the others. Sean sensed that the coins had no real connection to what was in the photo, yet when he held the picture, the image of the coins was as strong as anything he had ever felt psychically. And then he finally figured it out.

Sean grabbed a screwdriver and dismantled the frame. He pulled out the backing and, to his great joy, found what he had seen in his mind — two identical coins, both silver dollars. Holding them in his hand, he sensed they were worth a *lot* of money.

He was afraid to go to the coin shop out of fear that the dealer would try to take advantage of him because he was a kid. So Sean went to the library and thumbed through a price guide of coins. In the book was a photo of the coin that matched the two he had found — an 1893 S Morgan silver dollar. What he read next nearly caused him to faint. The coin, in mint condition, was worth $50,000! And he had two of them — both in mint condition!

* * *

Sean was in a daze. He hid the two coins in the toe of an old tennis shoe in his closet. Now he didn't know what to do.

He wanted to keep them. But then he thought about the last thing Crimmins had told him: "Read the coin. Then you'll know what to do." He pulled out Crimmins' bullet-dented silver dollar and tried to pick up new vibes. It was then that he saw a vision of a man Sean sensed was the only person Mr. Crimmins had trusted over the years. Sean recognized the man as one of only a handful of people who had attended Crimmins' funeral. He was Edward Pollard, a vice president of City National Bank.

The next day, Sean visited Pollard and they talked about the old man.

"I was Mr. Crimmins' banker since I first became an officer here in 1974," Pollard told Sean. "He was a sad, lonely man. Very strange. But he had a heart of gold. So you were his friend? Well then, I'm going to tell you something that's going to appear in tomorrow's newspaper.

"Money meant little to Mr. Crimmins personally. After his wife died, he had only one joy in his life — giving money away to charity without anyone else knowing about it, except me. He would sell off his rare coins and give me the money, which I would then anonymously donate to the worthy cause of his choice. It was always for children, because he never had kids of his own. Who do you think paid for the nursery for AIDS babies, the shelter for homeless families, and the building for the Boy's & Girl's Club? And who do you think helped keep the Parent-Child Center and the Children's Home Society running when they were in financial trouble? Mr. Crimmins. But he never wanted anybody to know. He swore me to secrecy.

"Now that he's dead, I think the community should know how generous he was. My one big regret is that I couldn't get Mr. Crimmins to write out a will. So now his nephew is selling off what's left of the coin collection and keeping the money for himself. I understand he's tearing up the place looking for money his uncle hid. And there should be money in the house either in cash or rare coins, because Mr. Crimmins told me he was about to make another big donation to help mentally-challenged children. My goodness, this has been a one-sided conversation. Can I help you with something?"

"You already have, Mr. Pollard." At that moment, Sean Davis thought about Crimmins' generosity, and the boy knew exactly what he was going to do with those two 1893 S Morgan silver dollars.

BLACKJACK'S RESCUE

For Jessica Miller's beloved dog Blackjack, it was a matter of life or death.

The black Labrador retriever lay dying deep in the woods, and no one knew where. Jessica realized there was only one hope of finding him in time — calling on the amazing psychic powers the teenager shared with her dog.

* * *

The moment Jessica laid eyes on Blackjack, she knew he was special. She just didn't know *how* special.

At the time, Jessica was a shy, overweight, eleven-year-old who suffered from a medical problem and didn't have many friends in school. Growing up in Macon, Georgia, she was a loner who spent most of her free time reading books and watching television.

Her parents thought Jessica should have a dog. They hoped that a puppy she could care for and train would help bring her out of her shell. So they took her to the local animal shelter to pick out a canine friend.

After peering in cage after cage, Jessica couldn't make up her mind between the barking beagle and the frisky terrier. "This is so hard to do," she said. "They're both so cute and cuddly. Okay, I choose —"

Suddenly, Jessica heard a strange inner voice say, *"The black puppy. The black puppy."* Of all the dogs she had seen that day, none were black. But then she turned around and noticed a shelter volunteer place a frightened, trembling black Labrador into a cage. When the puppy's brown eyes met Jessica's, he stopped shaking. His tail, which had been tucked between his legs, began wagging.

"Could I hold him, please?" she asked the volunteer. When Jessica held the puppy in her arms and felt his tongue slurp her chin, she fell instantly in love with him. "I swear he's telling me to choose him," she told her parents. "So I will. And I've got the perfect name for him — Blackjack."

Jessica's parents were right about getting a dog. With Blackjack as her four-footed companion, the girl's whole life changed. Jessica seemed so much more alive and happy. She began jogging in the morning with Blackjack, played Frisbee with him in the park, and swam with him in the lake. Blackjack was as eager to learn new tricks as Jessica was to teach them to him.

The dog was more than just a pet. He was her best friend. She could tell Blackjack anything and everything — things she could never confide to a teacher, counselor, or even her parents. Whenever she felt troubled or was trying to solve a problem, the dog would trot over to Jessica and put his head in her lap and listen — sometimes for hours.

He knew when to give her a sympathetic look, a wagging tail, or a knowing whine.

Jessica first sensed that she and Blackjack shared a psychic bond about a year after she adopted him.

Jessica had a disorder of the nervous system called epilepsy — a condition in which the brain gets short-circuited, causing the victim to shake uncontrollably for several seconds. Although Jessica took medication to treat the disorder, every once in awhile, especially when she was very tired, she would suffer a seizure.

One day, while Jessica was setting the table, Blackjack began barking in a high pitch she had never heard before. He kept running around her legs, stopping every so often to stare into her eyes.

"What's the matter with you, Blackjack?" she asked. "What's wrong?"

He yelped a few more times and then gently took her hand in his mouth and led her to the couch. Less than a minute later, Jessica suffered one of her seizures. From then on, Blackjack displayed the uncanny knack of predicting Jessica's epileptic seizures — something not even medical science could do! The dog would warn Jessica and her family of an impending seizure and lead her to a couch or bed so she wouldn't fall down and get hurt when she had a seizure.

This remarkable human-pet bond grew stronger over the next few years. Jessica found she didn't even have to talk out loud to communicate with Blackjack. If she thought about going for a walk, he would prance into her room with the leash in his mouth. If she felt depressed and wanted an emotional pick-me-up, Blackjack would nuzzle under her arm until she cracked a smile.

If Jessica concentrated, she could pick up psychic vibrations from Blackjack. She didn't need him to bark or whimper in order to know what he wanted or how he felt. She could tell. One time she sensed he was hurting, although there were no outward signs that he was sick or injured. So she took him to the veterinarian. Incredibly, the vet discovered the dog was suffering from an intestinal blockage that required an immediate operation.

Another time, during the middle of a math test, Jessica began thinking about Blackjack. She drifted off into a daydream-like trance, and what she saw in her mind made her laugh and moan at the same time.

"Blackjack!" she gasped.

"Shhh," said her teacher. "No talking."

"But my dog, he's gotten himself in a terrible mess!"

"Where? Is he right outside?"

"No, he's ... um ... I've got to go. Or he's going to be in worse trouble than he is now."

"Jessica, don't you dare leave this classroom," the teacher warned. The kids in the class started to giggle. But the feeling that Blackjack needed her was too strong to ignore. Jessica dashed out of the school and, without really knowing where she was headed, ended up a few blocks away in the backyard of Mrs. Holling. Scattered all over the lawn were sheets, blouses, underwear, and skirts that had been hanging up to dry. Two laundry lines had fallen down while a third one, holding sheets with muddy paw prints on them, was still standing. On top of the back porch were Mrs. Holling's two angry Siamese cats. With their backs arched and their hair on end, the cats were hissing at a howling, yelping Blackjack below.

"Oh, no! Blackjack! Look at this mess you've made!"

Jessica had forgotten to lock the gate to the Millers' fenced-in backyard. As a result, Blackjack sneaked out and roamed the neighborhood. Although he was the perfect pet — obedient, smart, and loving — he had one big fault. He went nuts when it came to rabbits, squirrels, and cats. He chased them no matter what, even if he were ordered to stay put. It was the only time he wouldn't obey. So when Blackjack spotted Mrs. Holling's cats napping in the elderly woman's backyard, he couldn't resist. He went after them with a vengeance, pursuing them around, over, and under the laundry lines. The cats finally leaped onto the porch roof for safety, but not before clothes were scattered in all directions.

As a punishment for forgetting to lock the Millers' backyard gate, Jessica had to wash and iron all of Mrs. Holling's laundry.

* * *

The strength of the psychic bond between the girl and her dog was tested like never before when Jessica visited her cousins in Jacksonville, Florida, for a week. It was the first time in the three years she owned Blackjack that she had left him behind for any length of time.

When her parents went to pick her up the following weekend, they decided to bring the dog with them and surprise Jessica.

Halfway through the five-hour drive to Jacksonville, the Millers stopped at a rest area and walked Blackjack. Suddenly, he spotted a squirrel and took off after it. No amount of shouting or pleading from the Millers could stop him. Blackjack galloped deep into the brush of a heavily wooded area until they couldn't hear him barking anymore. When he didn't return, the Millers began a search. But after an hour of walking through the woods and calling his name, they gave up. The heartbroken parents posted hand-scribbled notices on the bathroom doors of the rest area, offering a $50 reward.

Meanwhile, a hundred miles away, Jessica sensed that something was wrong. She had a vision that her dog was trapped and lost somewhere deep in the woods.

* * *

"One more hog and we'll call it a day," said Floyd Rymer as he and his fellow hunter Skip Noonan were tromping through the brush, looking to shoot another wild pig.

"Hey, over there," said Skip in a hushed tone. "What's that?" Through a thicket they could hear rustling in a near-by bush. Floyd peered through the dense brush and saw the short black hair of what he thought was a wild pig. He drew his rifle up, aimed, and fired. "Got him!"

The hunters hustled through the brush, pushed the branches aside, and stared down at their prey. But it wasn't a wild pig. It was Blackjack.

During the dog's wild squirrel chase, his collar had become entangled in the brambles of a bush. Blackjack was struggling to free himself when he was shot.

"You idiot!" Skip snarled at Floyd. "You shot a dog."

"Well, he shouldn't have been there. He should have barked or something."

Bleeding from a bullet wound in the head, the panic-stricken dog kept twisting and pulling his neck in a desperate effort to get away. With one final tug, he slipped out of his collar. Then he dashed off deeper into the woods.

"Whose dog was it?" asked Floyd.

Skip looked at the dog tag on the collar that Blackjack had left behind. "Someone named Miller in Macon."

"Well, that dog is gonna be a goner," said Floyd.

"Come on," muttered Skip. "Let's get out of here before you wind up shooting a cow."

* * *

Jessica's parents were devastated as they drove the rest of the way to Jacksonville without Blackjack. They talked about nothing else but the dog and their daughter. How were they going to break the news to Jessica that her dog had run away? How would she react? Would she ever get over it? Was there any hope that some nice person would find Blackjack and return him to them?

When they arrived in Jacksonville, they told Jessica what had happened. After a lengthy cry, Jessica declared, "We have to go back to the rest area. Either I'll find him or he'll find me."

Jessica didn't get any sleep that night. All she kept thinking about was her dog. She tried to stay calm, hoping to pick up psychic signals from Blackjack. Throughout the night she detected a feeling that he was lost and seriously hurt. But the message was fading with each passing hour.

Shortly before dawn, Jessica woke up her parents and begged them to drive her back to the rest area immediately.

"Blackjack's been calling for me all night," she told them. "He's dying. We've got to save him. There's no time to lose!"

* * *

Curtis Smith trudged in the woods with his trusty shovel, looking for mushrooms to dig up. It was a ritual the eighty-year-old former sheriff's deputy performed weekly at day-break throughout the spring.

"What the heck is that?" he asked out loud as he came across a bloodied dog sprawled out on the ground. Smith shook his head sadly as he bent down and examined the lifeless animal. *Can't find a pulse,* he thought. *Must be dead. Wonder whose it was. No collar. Haven't seen him around here. Isn't a stray. Looks too well-fed and cared for. A real shame. I should bury it.* So Smith dug a shallow grave, placed Blackjack in it, and covered him up with a few shovelfuls of dirt.

* * *

When Jessica and her parents arrived at the rest area, there was no sign of Blackjack. So they drove on the nearby back roads, stopping people along the way and asking if they had seen a lost black Labrador.

The last person they stopped was Floyd Rymer, who was carrying a rifle as he walked on the side of the road. "No, can't say as I've seen the dog," he told them. "Sorry."

As they started to drive off, Jessica shouted, "Daddy, stop! He's lying! He knows something about Blackjack!"

Her father hit the brakes and said, "Honey, you're not making any sense now because you're upset." Jessica flung open the car door and approached Floyd. She fumbled in her purse and pulled out all the money she had inside — five dollars — and dangled it in front of him.

"Please, Sir, think real hard. Have you seen a black dog wandering around here?"

"Look," said Floyd, getting irritated. "I told you I didn't see no dog, and I don't want your money." He grunted and walked off.

When Jessica returned to the car, she told her parents, "I got some strange vibes off of that man. He definitely knows where Blackjack is." She closed her eyes and spent a moment trying to clear her head so she could concentrate. She pointed to a nearby dirt road and said, "Let's go down there."

When the road ended, the Millers got out and followed a path into the woods. Jessica's heart started pounding faster. "We're on the right trail! I can feel it. Blackjack is around here somewhere!"

Moments later, Jessica screamed, "Mom, Dad, look!" Jammed in a thorny branch was Blackjack's collar. She bent down and, after a struggle, jerked it off the bush. Her hands began to tremble as she clutched his collar, because she began picking up psychic vibrations of terror, panic, confusion, and pain.

"Where is he?" she cried. "What's happened to him?"

Jessica then spotted dried blood by the bush, kneeled down, and touched it. "It has to be Blackjack's. He was here!" Closing her eyes again, she tried to send her dog a psychic message: *I'm here, Blackjack. Tell me where you are.*

Turning to her parents, she announced, "He's close. I know he's not dead. I can feel it. His heart is still beating."

Just then Curtis Smith, the retired deputy, approached the Millers. "Howdy, folks," he said.

"Sir," asked Jessica, "have you seen my black Labrador? He ran away and ..."

The old man put his hand on Jessica's shoulder and shook his head. "Missy, I am so sorry to tell you this. But I found a black Labrador a couple of hours ago, and he was already dead."

"No, he's not dead," sobbed Jessica. "He can't be."

"I'm afraid so, Missy. He got shot, probably by some careless hunter. I came across the dog this morning, lying there with no life in him. I looked for a pulse but couldn't find one. So I buried him right where he lay."

"Where, where?"

"Well, I don't know for sure," said Smith, scratching the gray stubble on his chin. "I was mushrooming and not paying much attention to exactly where I was. I hate to admit it, but I've been known to get turned around in these woods. Now let's see, I buried him not too far from here. I think if you go that way ..." He turned around and squinted. "Or is it that way?"

Jessica closed her eyes and concentrated on her dog. She didn't shout his name, she just called it in her mind. *Blackjack, Blackjack, where are you? Please, oh please, give me a sign. Tell me where you are.*

As though she were following some invisible guiding light, Jessica darted off into the brush. "This way!" she yelled. Weaving her way around the pines, brush, and brambles, she came to a small clearing and began scanning the ground, looking for some freshly dug earth. Falling to her knees, she crawled around, feeling the dirt to see where it was loose.

Suddenly, she froze. Out of the corner of her eye, she thought she saw some dirt move just a few feet away from her. *Am I seeing things? No, something is definitely pushing the dirt up from underneath.* "Here! Over here!" she shouted to her parents. Jessica frantically clawed at the earth and felt around. Could it be? Yes — a paw! Her parents raced over, helped uncover the dog, and pulled him free from his shallow grave. "Tell me you're alive, Blackjack!" urged Jessica. "Talk to me!"

Blackjack, his head covered in dried blood, opened his eyes and let out a whimper. "He's alive!" shouted Jessica. "He's alive!" She hugged her dog and cried until she was too weak to sob anymore. "Blackjack, oh, Blackjack, I love you!" He weakly licked her hand and wagged his tail.

As the Millers rushed Blackjack to the nearest animal clinic, Jessica held her dog on her lap and rocked back and forth in the back seat of the car. "Blackjack, hang on," she whispered, "Everything is going to be all right."

* * *

Dr. Mary Gladden, the local veterinarian, had finished cleaning Blackjack's wound and given him antibiotics and nutrients.

"Blackjack is going to be okay," she announced to the Millers. "That dog should have been dead. But he showed a strong will to survive and had a few lucky breaks. The bullet grazed his head. Another couple of inches and he would have been dead for sure. After he was shot, he ran until he collapsed and passed out. He had a very weak pulse. That's why Mr. Smith couldn't detect one. When he got buried, fortunately Mr. Smith didn't pack down the dirt, so there was enough air for Blackjack to breathe. It's amazing what this dog has gone through and survived. But what's even more incredible is that you people found him! It boggles the mind."

"It's not all that amazing," said Mr. Miller. "Not when you know how much love Blackjack and Jessica have for each other. They have a bond that goes beyond anything you and I could ever hope to understand."

DEADLY DREAMS

ost people hope their dreams come true.

But Anthony Russo didn't. Not after experiencing nightmares in which several relatives died.

Anthony never thought much about death. In fact, up until the age of ten, he had never been to a funeral because no one close to him had ever died. Both sets of his grandparents were still alive, and all his aunts and uncles were fairly young and healthy.

The Russos were an extremely close and large family who had been living in the south side of Chicago for generations, ever since Anthony's great-grandparents arrived from their homeland in Italy.

At least once a month, on a Sunday afternoon, the entire Russo family — grandparents, uncles, aunts, nephews, nieces, and cousins — would gather at one of their houses. There they would play cards, cheer whichever Chicago sports team was playing on television, and eat homemade spaghetti, ravioli, and lasagna. They would dine in shifts, the kids first and then the adults. If the weather was nice, they would all sit around card tables in the backyard and eat until their stomachs were ready to burst.

Anthony loved those Sundays because of the food, fun, and fights that accompanied every gathering. Uncle Manny and Uncle Louie would argue over politics until Anthony feared the debate would flare into a fistfight. Uncle Sal and the kids would try to outdo each other with terrible jokes. Nana and Poppa — that's what the grandparents were called — would sit in their easy chairs and tell thrilling stories of the days when machine-gun-toting gangsters ruled the streets of Chicago. And everywhere, shouts of laughter and curses filled the air. But by the end of the day, those who had argued had kissed and made up. It was one big, happy family.

Then came the dream that changed Anthony's life.

One night, shortly after one of the family gatherings, Anthony experienced a terrible nightmare. It wasn't scary with monsters or goblins. It was troubling and dark and very sad. In his dream, he watched an old woman dressed in a long black coat with a black scarf over her head slowly walk down a lonely city sidewalk on a foggy night. She cast an eerie shadow from the light of a lone street lamp and walked with a slight shuffle and the aid of a cane.

The old woman stumbled and fell, and Anthony rushed to her side. But she held up her hand and signaled him to back off. She turned her head away so he wouldn't see her, but Anthony caught a glimpse of her face. It was Nana. He reached out to her, but she gently brushed away his hand. "No, no, I must do this alone," she said in a determined voice. She struggled to her feet and continued her walk. "I must go, it's my time."

"Go?" asked Anthony. "Where?"

"I have lived all that I can live," replied Nana. "I must go now. Look after Poppa for me. I love you, *mio carissimo* [my dear one]."

Anthony tried to go after her, but some force kept him rooted at the street corner. All he could do was helplessly watch Nana disappear into the swirling night fog. When he sensed that she would never come back, he broke into heavy sobs.

"Anthony! Anthony! What's wrong?"

His younger brother Mike, who slept in the bunk bed below him, was shaking Anthony.

"Huh?" gurgled Anthony as he opened his eyes.

"Are you okay?" asked Mike.

Once he cleared his head, Anthony realized his face and pillow were soaked with tears. "I had this awful dream," he said. "It was about Nana. I can't explain it, but I had this real sad feeling about her like I'm never going to see her again."

"Man, don't talk like that," said Mike. "You had a nightmare, that's all. Just a bad dream." Mike climbed into his bunk and went back to sleep.

But Anthony couldn't sleep. All he kept thinking about was Nana. He wanted to rush to the phone and call her, but it was only 4:30 in the morning. He didn't dare wake up Nana and Poppa that early. He'd just have to wait until the morning.

For the next hour, Anthony lay in bed and recalled all the wonderful times he had spent with Nana. During the holidays, she would take him on the el, the elevated train, to downtown Chicago to see all the decorations, especially the four-story-tall Christmas tree inside Marshall Field's, the department store. On hot summer nights, she would give him a lesson in speaking Italian as they walked from her apartment to a nearby stand where she bought her grandson *granita,* flavored Italian ice. She would take Anthony to the Museum of Science and Industry and ask him to explain to her the new exhibits because she had such a thirst for knowledge even though she had never finished high school. Those were great times, and Anthony didn't ever want them to end.

He tried to tell himself that the dream was nothing, just one of those rare nightmares. But in his heart, he couldn't convince himself. *Oh, why isn't it morning yet?* He checked the clock. *It's only 5:42. It's still too early to call.*

* * *

"Anthony, Michael, wake up, kids," said their mother as she stuck her head into their room.

"Huh, what time is it?" Anthony asked groggily.

"Almost eight," she replied. "Would you both please get up and come downstairs. We need to talk."

The tone in her voice told Anthony that something was wrong, terribly wrong. His heart sank when he noticed that his mother's eyes were red and puffy.

Anthony leaped down from the bunk bed. His knees were shaking with dread, and his stomach hurt from the worry of what he was about to hear. Part of him wanted to run down the stairs and part of him didn't want to move. Somehow, he felt that when he reached the kitchen, his life would change forever.

Sitting at the table, his mother Rose and his father Leonard stared blankly at the wall, each clutching a handkerchief. They obviously had been crying.

"Boys," said their dad, trying hard to hold back the tears, "we have some very, very bad news."

"Oh, no!" Anthony gasped. "It's Nana, isn't it?" His lips began to tremble, and tears streamed down his face.

"Yes, son, I'm afraid it is," Leonard replied in a cracking voice. "Nana died sometime during the night in her sleep. We got the call about an hour ago from Poppa. He couldn't wake her up for their morning walk. So he phoned the paramedics and then called me. I rushed over to the apartment, but the paramedics said there was nothing they could do. They think she died of a heart attack." His father started to cry again.

"May she rest in peace," Rose murmured.

"Not Nana!" Anthony cried out. "Oh, please tell me I'm still having a dream — a very bad dream!"

After the family had run out of tears, Leonard asked his son, "Anthony, how did you know it was Nana before I had told you?"

"I had a nightmare last night, Dad. Nana was in it, and she told me she had to go. I just had this feeling that something really bad was going to happen, but I didn't know what it was." Anthony began to shudder again, this time out of a combination of heartache for the loss of his beloved grandmother and shock that his awful dream of her death had actually come true.

By the end of the day, everyone in the Russo family had heard about Anthony's dream. Some relatives tried to tell him it was just coincidence. Others pooh-poohed it because, after all, Nana hadn't died in his dream. She just walked off in the foggy night. But many of his aunts and uncles were convinced it was a psychic dream. They tried to pump him for every bit of information they could. "What else did Nana say?" "Did she leave any message for me?" "Was she at peace?" "Was she afraid?"

It was too much for Anthony. He bolted outside and ran as hard as he could for as long as he could until his lungs were ready to burst. When he returned home, he went into the kitchen and saw an official piece of paper on the table. It was the death certificate. Under the box marked time of death, the doctor wrote "between 3 and 5 A.M." Only then did it dawn on Anthony that he had awakened from his dream at 4:30 A.M.

For the next several weeks, Anthony went to bed wondering if he would have another dream about Nana. But he never did. Eventually, he stopped thinking about the nightmare, although Nana was never far from his thoughts.

About a year after Nana's death, Anthony experienced another horrible nightmare. This time, he was at a wake in a funeral home. Everyone was dressed in black and crying. In the front of the room, under a spotlight, was an open, highly polished, wooden coffin surrounded by flowers. Anthony couldn't make out the identity of the body.

As the boy walked toward the casket, he could hear words of shock from grief-stricken relatives.

"It's so hard to believe he's gone."

"I was talking to him the night before he died."

"Things like this aren't supposed to happen."

"I'll miss him so much."

Anthony still didn't know who they were talking about

until he reached the coffin and looked down. It was Salvatore Russo, his favorite uncle!

Anthony jumped back. "No, not Uncle Sal!" he shouted to the mourners in the room. "This can't be happening! He's the strongest and healthiest of them all. How could he be dead?"

When Anthony woke up the next morning, he raced downstairs. "Mom! Dad! I'm really worried about Uncle Sal. I think something really bad is going to happen to him."

"Son," said his father. "Uncle Sal is having a simple knee operation, the kind performed on lots of athletes. It's routine surgery. He'll be fine."

"But I dreamed that Uncle Sal *died*!" Anthony said with alarm. "I saw him in a coffin and..."

"Anthony, don't talk like that," said his mother.

"But I dreamed it," he insisted. "I don't want this dream to come true like it did for Nana. Promise me it won't. Promise me Uncle Sal will be all right."

"You're probably just worried about Uncle Sal," said his father. "After all, you're pretty close to him, and you've probably been thinking about him. He's in surgery right now. In an hour, he'll be out. We'll go over to the hospital, and you'll see he's just fine."

Anthony tried to watch TV, hoping it would take his mind off the nightmare, but it didn't. He kept thinking about Uncle Sal.

Forty-year-old Salvatore Russo coached his son Sal, Jr. and Anthony in the church basketball league and enjoyed taking the boys to White Sox games where he would yell his head off, sometimes to the kids' embarrassment. He had a quick smile and a ready joke for everyone he met while on the job for the city street department. Young at heart, Sal spent more time with the kids than with the adults at the Russo family gatherings. He always told the worst jokes, but because they were so bad the kids laughed anyway. Sal had gone into the hospital for surgery on his knee, which he had injured during a pickup basketball game.

Anthony had been watching TV for about an hour when the telephone rang. His heart sank because he knew, *he just knew*, that the call would confirm his worst fears about his Uncle Sal. Scrambling to his feet, Anthony yelled, "No, Mom! Don't answer the phone! It's going to be bad news!"

It was too late.

"Oh, my God!" his mother cried out. "I don't believe what I'm hearing!" She slumped down into the kitchen chair with her hand over her mouth in shock. Weakly, she hung up the phone and burst into tears.

"Is it about Uncle Sal?" asked Anthony, hoping against hope he was wrong.

"Yes, Anthony," she said, pulling him toward her to give her son a comforting hug. "He died this morning. Something went wrong on the operating table while he was being put under with an anesthetic. The doctors don't know what happened. He just died..." She began weeping uncontrollably.

Once again, Anthony's dream of death had come true.

For weeks afterwards, Anthony was afraid to go to sleep because he was scared he would dream about another loved one who would die. He read action comic books into the wee hours of the morning hoping that if he filled his mind with super heroes, his brain would be too crowded to dream of his relatives. Staying up late night after night until he was overcome by exhaustion caused Anthony to suffer from depression and several minor stomach problems.

But with loving understanding from his parents and a professional therapist, Anthony eventually came to grips with his deadly dreams. Maybe he did have a psychic ability to foretell the death of a loved one. Maybe it was nothing but coincidence. Either way, he had to accept it because there was nothing he could do.

* * *

Two years went by before Anthony experienced another nightmare — this one involving his cousin Gino, a student at the University of Michigan. Gino, five years older than Anthony, acted like an older brother. Because the two loved sports, Gino would give him tips on playing football, basketball, and baseball. A popular, happy-go-lucky young man, Gino worked during the summer as a lifeguard at the neighborhood YMCA and as a camp counselor.

In his deadly dream, Anthony once again showed up at a wake, only this time for Gino. But it wasn't held at a funeral home. It was in the home of his Uncle Manny and Aunt Sue, Gino's parents. Anthony noticed something very odd. No one was crying. In fact, everyone was laughing, drinking, and eating like they were at a party. Yet it was still a wake. With Gino dead, Anthony couldn't understand why nobody seemed to care.

As he walked around the room, Anthony heard his relatives talking.

"Isn't it great?"

"Oh, what a relief."

"I can't believe it."

"It could only happen to Gino."

Everybody loved Gino, thought Anthony. *Why would they react to his death like this?*

Shortly before daybreak, Anthony woke up from his dream heartsick and frantic. He charged into his parents' bedroom and shook them awake.

"Mom! Dad! I had another one of those death dreams," he wailed.

"Oh, no," gasped his mother. "Who is it this time?"

"It's Gino, Mom. I dreamed I was at his wake."

His mother clutched her heart and began to cry.

"But there was something really weird about it," said Anthony. "Everyone was laughing and having a good time. Even you, Dad. What does it mean?"

"I don't have the foggiest idea," his father replied. "I don't understand why you have these dreams. But since the first two turned out to be true, we can't ignore this one. Maybe the dream is a warning, and we can phone Gino and tell him to be extra careful today."

But even though it was only 6 A.M., there was no answer at Gino's dormitory room. Anthony was on pins and needles all day, waiting for the news that his cousin had died. Word came later that afternoon. There had been a terrible boating accident on Lake Michigan, authorities told Gino's parents, Manny and Sue. Gino had borrowed a motorboat to go fishing. But a few miles out on the lake, the boat had caught fire and exploded. Gino had died.

All the members of the Russo family were crushed by the news, especially Anthony, who was too numb from sorrow to even cry. Tragically, the first part of his dream had come true. But for the life of him, he couldn't figure out how the second part — the happy wake — could happen. How could anyone party after Gino's shocking death? The answer would come later that evening.

"Gino's alive!" shouted Anthony's father. "Gino's alive!" Anthony, his mom, and his brother Michael crowded around the phone as Leonard relayed the conversation he was having with Gino's dad. When he hung up the phone, Leonard hugged his wife and kids and excitedly told them the wonderful news.

"It seems that Gino was having some engine problems about ten miles out in the lake. The engine finally conked out on him, and another boat passed by and gave him a lift. For whatever reason — they think there was a short-circuit in the wiring — Gino's boat exploded. But he was already a few miles away when it happened, and he didn't know about the blast. Just his luck, the boat that picked him up lost its propeller.

"By the time they radioed in for help, the marine patrol was out searching the water for Gino's body. There was a mix-up in communications, and someone called Manny and Sue and told them that Gino had died in a boating accident. Gino didn't know anything about it until he got back to shore about five hours later. That's when he learned he had 'died.' When Manny and Sue showed up, they all had one big happy cry!" Now it was the Leonard Russo family's turn to have one.

A week later, the second part of Anthony's death dream came true — and it all made perfectly logical sense. Gino returned home from college for the weekend to attend a big party thrown by his parents, who were ever so thankful their son was alive. All the Russos arrived to celebrate Gino's "death" — exactly like Anthony had dreamed!

DEAD
AGAIN

anessa Simpson didn't understand what was
happening. She was staring at an uncon-
scious girl who lay in the street. The girl's
limbs all pointed in a different direction like
those of a rag doll that had been flung aside.
A few feet away, a mangled bicycle rested
underneath a pickup truck.

What made this tragic scene so mind-numbing for
Vanessa was that the severely injured girl was none other
than Vanessa herself!

* * *

Vanessa, nine, and her sisters Latoya, eleven, and
Tamika, twelve, had hopped on their bikes to go to the nearby convenience store for some treats. Vanessa felt so proud
that day. She was riding her very own three-speed road bike
for the first time. It didn't matter that it had been bought by
her father at a police auction of abandoned property. So
what if the scratched-up blue bicycle once belonged to

somebody else? It was hers now — a road bike just like the older kids had.

But the big-eyed girl didn't exactly ride like the older kids. With her pigtails flopping back and forth, Vanessa wobbled down the street on her bike because her bony arms and legs barely reached the handlebars and pedals. She wasn't yet accustomed to the turned-down handlebars, the thin tires, and the hand brakes. Her old bike was smaller, had high-rise handlebars, thick tires, and a foot brake.

It had rained earlier in the day, so the streets were somewhat slick. The three Simpson sisters, trying to be careful cyclists, rode single file on the right side of the street all the way to the store. They each bought a candy bar and then headed for the park a few blocks from their home. Tamika took the lead, followed by Latoya and Vanessa.

On the way, Vanessa heard loud chattering and chirping coming from an oak tree branch that extended out over the street in front of her. As she rode under the tree, Vanessa looked up and spotted an irate robin pecking at a squirrel who had edged too close to the bird's nest. Vanessa kept her eyes glued to the tree, watching the drama unfold. But she didn't realize she had strayed out into the middle of the street.

At that moment, a pickup truck emerged from an alley and turned directly into her path. The driver honked his horn and slammed on his brakes. Vanessa was so startled that she forgot she was riding a road bike instead of her old bicycle. She instantly backpedaled, but that did nothing to slow her down. In her panic, Vanessa forgot about using her hand brakes. She tried to swerve out of the way, but she jerked too hard and lost her balance.

"Vanessa!" Tamika cried out. "Look out!"

The pickup skidded only a few feet before striking Vanessa as she was falling. The truck then ran over her and her bike before it could stop.

For a brief moment, Vanessa felt nothing at all except her face pressed firmly against the rough concrete surface of the street. Then pain stabbed her everywhere — her head, her arms, and her legs. She had never felt such intense pain in her life. Unable to move or talk, Vanessa could do nothing but listen to the hysterical screams of her sisters and shouts of anguish from stunned witnesses.

"Call 911!" shouted the horrified driver.

"My sister! My sister!" wailed Latoya as she staggered in shock.

Tamika took one look at Vanessa's nearly lifeless body and fell to her knees. "This can't be happening! Vanessa! Say something, please, say something!"

"Anyone have a blanket?" a man shouted as a crowd formed around the stricken girl. In the distance, sirens from a police car and an ambulance grew louder.

Then everything fell dark and silent for Vanessa.

Slowly but steadily, the pain eased until it vanished and was replaced by a wonderfully comforting feeling of peacefulness. Vanessa felt herself leaving her body and floating up in the air. And she could see again.

Invisible and hovering about ten feet above the accident scene, Vanessa didn't know what had happened. Her brain swirled with questions. *Where am I? Why am I floating like this? Why is the ambulance here? Who are all those people? Why are my sisters crying? Who's that lying in the street?*

Vanessa floated over the crowd and peered down at the

victim sprawled on the street. *Why, that's me! What's going on? I don't understand.* And suddenly it no longer mattered. Her questions and concerns vanished in an instant. She felt no heartache about what she was witnessing, only warmth and peace as though she were snug in her pajamas watching her favorite TV show without a care in the world.

Not so for the paramedics, who were engaged in a life-or-death scene crackling with tension, emotion, and desperation.

"I'm still not getting any pulse!" shouted one of the medics.

"Keep up the CPR!" replied his partner.

"Save her!" screamed Tamika. "You've got to save her!"

Vanessa began feeling a strange force pulling her back toward her body. As she moved closer to her body, the pain in her head, arms, and legs grew in intensity. There was no stopping the force, and she slipped back into her body. Once again, she experienced horrible pain and cold and darkness.

"I've got a pulse!" the paramedic cried.

"Radio the hospital," his partner ordered the ambulance driver. "Tell them we're bringing in a girl with severe trauma to the head, possible internal injuries, and probable broken legs and arms!"

Vanessa was rushed straight into the operating room, where a team of doctors and nurses worked feverishly to stabilize her, but without much success at first.

"We're having a problem with her vital signs, doctor!"

"Blood pressure is dropping!"

"We have cardiac arrest!"

"Start CPR immediately!"

For the second time, Vanessa found herself leaving her body and floating, this time above the surgical table. Free from pain and bathed in warmth, she looked down and saw herself hooked up by wires and tubes to various machines and monitors. From her vantage point above, she watched the doctors and nurses, clad in green scrubs and booties, scurry about in a furious effort to save the life of their patient.

In her haste, one nurse accidentally knocked over a tray of surgical instruments. "What a klutz I am," said the nurse. "I'll bring another tray immediately, doctor."

A few minutes later, the surgeon backed away from the operating table. "I've got to stop for a moment," he said. "My contact lens slipped down into the corner of my eye. I'm blind as a bat in that eye without it." A nurse used her finger to move the contact back into position.

Slowly, a mysterious force pulled Vanessa away from the operating room and into a tunnel of glowing silver clouds. She felt herself drifting like a leaf in a gentle breeze. It reminded her of that scene in *Alice in Wonderland* when Alice fell down the rabbit hole, only this was in slow motion and she was drifting up through the tunnel. As she reached the other end, Vanessa moved effortlessly toward a white light that grew ever brighter — brighter than the sun on the clearest day. Yet it wasn't blinding. It was comforting. As she reached the end of the tunnel, Vanessa felt at total peace. And in that instant, she knew everything would turn out all right, whatever her fate.

The force began tugging at her again, pulling her away from the light and back into the tunnel. Vanessa didn't want to leave the warm, comfortable peacefulness of the white light, but she allowed herself to float down through the silvery tunnel and into the operating room.

Vanessa didn't go back into her body, however. She hovered over the surgical table while the doctors finished operating. Then, realizing she could float through walls, she followed her body as the nurses below wheeled her into the intensive care unit.

She floated into the waiting room where she saw her heartsick parents and her tearful sisters talking to the surgeon, Dr. Gerald Stein.

"Vanessa has suffered a severe injury to the head," he told them. "Her heart stopped beating twice, once at the accident scene and again on the operating table. Luckily, we got it started. She's in very serious condition and in a coma right now. I'll be honest with you. She may not make it through the night. There's not much else we can do at this point except wait and hope."

"My baby! My baby!" her mother Ida wailed. "You can't let her die, doctor. She's so young."

Vanessa wanted to reach out and tell her family not to cry, that she would be all right. But she couldn't do anything except float around the room, invisible to everyone, and observe.

"I wish I had never bought her that bicycle," moaned her father, Henry. "I should have made her stay close to home and practice riding it before we let her go out in the street."

"Don't blame yourself," said Ida. "It won't do any good."

Tamika and Latoya stared blankly at each other. "Do you think that if she gets well, she'll ever be able to jump rope again?" asked Tamika. "I mean, for her age, she was the best. No one could do the double cartwheel like

Vanessa." She started to cry. "And who's going to take care of Bart? That cat hates all of us except Vanessa. Remember when she found him in the alley? He was nothing but skin and bones and had fleas, and Daddy wouldn't allow him in the house. She'd feed him and sneak him in her bed and then get up before Daddy did and let him out."

"I don't know what I'd do without Vanessa," said Latoya, her voice weary from crying. "I'd miss all those nights we'd try to scare each other with ghost stories. And I wouldn't be able to tease her about those stupid cheese-and-sugar sandwiches she makes. And who else could I make giggle in church? She'd crack up at anything. Vanessa can't die, she just can't." Latoya clasped her hands over her mouth. "What will happen to me if she dies without knowing the truth about her sweater? I secretly borrowed it, even though she asked me not to, and got that grape-juice stain on it."

"I've got a confession to make, too," admitted Tamika. "I was the one who broke her music box, not the cat like I told her."

A nurse carrying a big envelope walked over to their mother. "Mrs. Simpson, I brought you Vanessa's things."

On the waiting-room couch, Ida gently dumped out the contents — two barrettes, hoop earrings, a dainty gold necklace Vanessa had received from her grandparents on her eighth birthday, eighty-seven cents in change, a colorful friendship bracelet, and a broken watch with the hands frozen at 10:38 A.M. — the exact time of the accident. "Henry, do you think she'll ever get to wear these things again?" Then Ida collapsed in her husband's arms and sobbed.

If only Vanessa could communicate with her family. If

only she could put her arms around them and tell them she felt at peace and that they should remain strong. But she was powerless. Try as she might, she couldn't make any contact with them. But she hoped that maybe, just by being there, they'd feel some comfort from her presence even though she was invisible to them.

Suddenly everything went black for Vanessa. She was no longer floating. Instead, the force had thrust her back into her comatose body. Eventually, Vanessa began dreaming repeatedly about those final seconds before the accident: the robin and the squirrel … the honking pickup truck … the backpedaling … the collision … the screams … the pain.

Pain of all kinds — stabbing, throbbing, and aching — ravaged Vanessa throughout her body. Only now it wasn't a dream. She could feel the I.V. needles in her arms, the tube down her throat, and oxygen flowing up her nose. She groaned.

"Did you hear that, Henry?" Ida asked excitedly. "I heard her groan. Listen."

Vanessa groaned again. "Baby, baby, can you hear me?" asked her mother, squeezing her daughter's hand. Vanessa squeezed back weakly and managed to utter "uh-huh."

"Glory be, she's coming out of the coma!" shouted Ida. "Call the doctor!"

Vanessa had been in a coma for nearly a day. But in a remarkable recovery that amazed her doctors, she began breathing and drinking liquids on her own within four days of the accident. And she showed no signs of any permanent brain damage.

"You're a remarkable girl," Dr. Stein told her. "You showed a strong will to live."

"You thought I wouldn't make it," she stated. "I heard you tell that other doctor I had a ten percent chance of surviving."

"When did you hear this?"

"When you and he were walking to the waiting room after my operation."

"But how did you know? You were still in the operating room."

"I was floating outside my body, Dr. Stein. I could see and hear everything during and after the operation. You were working on my heart and got it going again. I watched you operate on me, and it looked pretty yucky.

"Child, what are you talking about?" asked her mother. "That head injury has got you saying wild things."

"No, Mrs. Simpson, let her go on," said Dr. Stein. "Vanessa is not the first patient who's told me about having an out-of-body experience. What else did you see, Vanessa?"

"Well, I saw a nurse knock over a tray of instruments and she called herself a klutz. And then you had to stop in the middle of the operation because you had a problem with your contact lens."

"You're absolutely right," said the doctor.

"Maybe she heard the tray drop and heard you talk about your contact," said Vanessa's father, who refused to believe his daughter's outrageous story about leaving her body and floating in the air.

"You could be right, Mr. Simpson," said Dr. Stein. "But then again... Go on, Vanessa."

She told them about the silvery tunnel and the wondrous bright light, leaving her parents shaking their heads in bewilderment. "It must be the medication," declared her father. "She probably dreamed all this during her coma."

"It was real, Daddy," Vanessa insisted. "I visited you in the waiting room. You were kicking yourself for buying me that bike and, Momma, you were crying real hard after the nurse handed you an envelope with all my things in it. And you wondered if I'd ever be able to wear those things again."

When Vanessa finished describing what she had seen and heard while floating in the waiting room, her parents were flabbergasted. "Doctor," said Mr. Simpson. "If this is all true, you might have to prescribe something for me to calm my nerves."

"Whether you want to believe it or not, her story is not that unusual," said Dr. Stein. "Many people who have a near-death experience are able to provide accurate details about their operation. They have described things about what they saw and heard even though they were unconscious at the time, had lost all their vital signs, and were clinically dead like Vanessa was."

"But," said Ida Simpson, "this seems so, so…"

"Unbelievable?" said Dr. Stein. "Look, I don't try to explain these experiences. But I'm willing to accept them. Unfortunately, science is quick to dismiss things when it doesn't have a ready answer."

Shortly after the doctor left, Latoya and Tamika came into the room for the first time to sit with Vanessa while their parents went to grab a bite to eat. "Is there anything we can do for you?" Tamika asked.

"Yes," answered Vanessa with a sly grin. "You can buy me a new music box. And Latoya, from now on, I get to borrow any sweater of yours whenever I want!"

THE TRAIN OF DOOM

T he grinding of metal ... the feeling of plunging into water ... and everywhere the sounds of moans, whimpers, and sobs.

For two straight nights, those vivid images and sounds haunted the nightmares of twelve-year-old Marco Martinez. He didn't understand their meaning — until it was almost too late.

* * *

Normally, the happy, dark-haired fifth-grader would have been thrilled at the chance to go with his grandmother on a cross-country train trip. But as he boarded the train in Los Angeles on a Sunday night for the three-day journey to New York City, Marco was filled with dread. And he didn't know why.

He didn't dare say anything to Abuelita — that's what he called his grandmother — because she was using some of the insurance money from her husband's recent death to pay for the trip. She wanted her oldest grandchild to view the beautiful, ever-changing landscape of the United States by rail. And she wanted him to meet the relatives in New York whom he had never met.

There wasn't much to see at night after the train pulled out of Los Angeles and clickety-clacked its way east. So Marco and his grandmother pushed their recliner seats back and went to sleep.

Once again, he experienced that same nightmare — the grinding metal, the plunge, and screams of terror. But this time, the frightening dream added a new element — people drowning. The nightmare seemed so real that he let out a shout so loud it woke him up.

"Marco! What's wrong?" asked his startled grandmother.

"Abuelita, I had a horrible nightmare. It was awful."

"Maybe it was the terrible food we ate at the train station," she said with a grin.

"No, Abuelita, I've had this nightmare before. In fact, I've had it the last two nights. And I've been having these weird feelings about this trip. Do you think there's any connection?"

She stroked his thick black hair and said, "Your bad dreams mean nothing. We all get them from time to time. It's best to ignore them. Oh, look. See the moon rising over that mountain? Isn't it beautiful?"

Marco wanted to get those haunting, nightmarish images out of his mind. But he couldn't — not after what he overheard at breakfast the next morning in the dining car. He took a quick glance at the husky teenage boy, who looked about sixteen, sitting behind him. The boy was talking in a hushed but very excited tone. His arms were gesturing wildly as he spoke to his parents.

"Man, like this dream was so real. I mean, people were dying and everything. They were trapped inside the train and they were trying to claw their way out the back, and the water was rising faster and faster. And pretty soon it was up to their necks and then I didn't see or hear anything. Is that freaky or what?"

He's had the same dream as me! thought Marco. *I've got to talk to him!*

Shortly after breakfast, Marco followed the teen to the lounge car, where many passengers gathered to play cards. "I like your Metallica T-shirt," said Marco.

"Thanks," the teen replied. "They're a great group."

"My name is Marco Martinez."

"Hi, I'm Justin Thomas. Where are you headed?"

"New York. What about you?"

"The same."

"Uh, Justin, I don't know how to say this, but I couldn't help but overhear your conversation this morning at breakfast. You were talking about a dream. Is it true you dreamed about people drowning?"

"Yeah, so what about it?" Justin sounded a bit annoyed that his private conversation with his parents had been overheard.

"I've had the same bad dream — last night and two times before that."

"Really? Cool." Justin pulled him aside and whispered, "Have you ever heard of clairvoyance?"

"No," Marco replied.

"It means predicting the future. Do you have dreams that come true?"

"I dreamed the Dodgers would win the World Series in 1988, and that was before the season even started. They won it, too."

"No, man, like dreaming about car wrecks and plane crashes before they happen," said Justin. "I hardly ever remember my dreams, but when I get them, they're doozies. I once dreamed I was in a big box, and a giant hand was shaking it real hard. The next day, we had an earthquake."

Marco's eyes lit up and he said, "I had one where I was walking through the house of my buddy Jose Cabrerra, but it was all charred and smokey and everyone was crying. And believe it or not, his house burned down a couple of days later."

"Get a load of this," said Justin, his voice full of drama. "I was riding with some buddies in the back seat of a car when I saw — like, right in my mind — a huge boulder come crashing down the hill and smash into a car. Not more than two minutes later we went around a curve and there was a car all squashed from a boulder. Man, did that freak me out!"

"The dreams on the train. Does that mean we're clair … clair …"

"Clairvoyant. Could be. Maybe these dreams are trying to tell us something. But I'm not quite sure what. Hey, if you get any more nightmares, tell me. And I'll do the same for you."

* * *

At lunch, Marco and his grandmother sat with an elderly couple, the Lansings, who were heading back home to New York. As sweet and pleasant as they were, Marco didn't pay much attention to them at first. He'd smile and answer their questions politely, but his mind was drifting elsewhere — to his nightmare and his conversation with Justin. But then Marco started getting strong feelings about the Lansings. Feelings of terror and death. It seemed to hang over them like a thick cloud.

After the Lansings had left, Marco held his grandma's arm and said, "Abuelita, I have such a terrible feeling about them ... about the train ... about us. I'm all mixed up and I don't know what to think." He then told her about the feeling of death he had for the Lansings and about Justin's nightmare.

"What am I going to do with you?" asked his annoyed grandmother. "Here I spend lots of money so you can take a trip with me to New York and see the countryside, and all you do is whine about some nightmare. You're missing this great traveling experience. Now stop it, please You're going to ruin this trip for yourself and for me."

Midway through the night, Marco experienced another horrifying dream. It was more detailed, more real: passengers hurled out of their seats ... the train car falling off a bridge into the water and sinking ... blood-curdling screams ... people shouting for help. "We're all going to die!" "Please help me, I'm drowning!"

Tossing and turning, Marco bellowed out "Noooo!" so loud that he woke up several passengers, including himself.

"Marco, are you having another nightmare?" asked his alarmed grandmother.

"Oh, Abuelita, this one was even worse. It's definitely

this train! There's going to be an accident, and people in our car are going to die! I know it. I just know it."

"Where are you getting these awful ideas? From that boy you met on the train, right? Stay away from him. He's been putting crazy thoughts into your head. You have to stop this, I beg of you. You're driving me *loco*."

The next morning, as he walked to the dining car with his grandmother, Marco slipped a note to Justin, who was just waking up. "Meet me at eight in the last car," said the note.

* * *

When Justin walked into the last coach, Marco excitedly told him, "I had another nightmare last night. The train fell off a bridge, and people were splashing around in the water and crying for help."

"Hey, dude, I'm getting really freaked," said Justin, his eyes growing wide. "I had almost the same dream! I told my parents, and they think my imagination is working overtime. This is so bizarre. Do you have any idea when or where this accident will happen?"

"It was getting dark in my dream," replied Marco. "And I remember there were lots of big ships nearby."

"A harbor maybe."

"What can we do?" asked Marco.

"The conductor isn't going to do anything, so we can't talk to him," Justin replied. "It probably won't do any good to pull the emergency brake. All that will do is get us in trouble. Besides, we don't know when to pull it. Ten minutes from now? Ten hours from now? The train will stop, they'll find out we did it, we'll be in major trouble, and then the train will go on its way." He threw up his hands in surrender and then added, "There's something else to consider."

"What's that?"

"We could be wrong."

But Marco was convinced otherwise. After Justin left, Marco looked at a map of the train route and tried to figure out the most likely place for the crash based on his and Justin's nightmares. The only major harbors on the route were between Philadelphia and New York City. *So that must mean the crash is going to happen tonight somewhere between those two cities!* thought Marco.

He ran back to his train car and whispered his theory to Justin, who had a strange look on his face. "Hey, dude, listen to me, okay," said Justin, nervously glancing at his parents next to him. "I've been pulling your chain. It was a practical joke. I made up all that stuff about the dreams. I was just having some fun with you, that's all."

"But I heard you talking to your parents."

"I was kidding them. And then you popped into the picture, so I decided to have some fun with you. I got carried away, and I figured I'd play it for all it was worth. Maybe even get you to pull the emergency brake. Hey, I really had you going there, didn't I?"

"You're a jerk!"

"I'm sorry, man, okay? Stay cool. There isn't going to be any crash."

Marco walked away, stunned. The only person who shared his belief of impending doom was a fraud. *A punk, nothing but a punk who had a good laugh at my expense,* he thought. *Now I have no one who believes me.*

Every minute meant the train was one mile closer to Philadelphia. Marco stared glumly out the window as the train sped past Pittsburgh and through the rolling hills of western Pennsylvania. *I've got to think of something,* thought Marco. *The next stop is Harrisburg and then Philadelphia. If I can't save people on the train, at least I can save Abuelita and myself. But how? I could pretend I'm sick. That's it! Yeah, then she'll get me off the train.*

"Oh, Abuelita, I don't feel so good."

"What's wrong, Marco?"

"My stomach. I have real bad pains in my stomach."

"You didn't touch your lunch, and you hardly ate any breakfast. That's why you've got a stomachache."

"No, it's worse than that. Ohhh," he groaned. He grabbed the left side of his stomach. "I think it's my appendix."

"It's not your appendix."

"How do you know?"

"Because your appendix is on the right side. Marco Luis Torres Martinez, I've known you from the time you took your first breath, and I've never heard you lie to me. Now tell me the truth. Are you really in pain?"

When he hesitated, she hissed, "You must stop playing these games." His grandmother rubbed her face in bewilderment and sighed. "You and that boy back there," she said, pointing to Justin in the rear of the car. "His parents are pretty upset with him, too, you know. I heard them tell him to stop all this nonsense about a train wreck. Marco, I don't know what I'm going to do with you. Maybe we should get off the train at the next stop so I can send you back to Los Angeles."

"Yes, yes, please. But only if you come with me. You can't stay on the train. It's going to crash sometime tonight after we get to Philadelphia."

"This from a boy who thought he was poisoned from eating a homemade cookie on Halloween and ran home hysterical after only four houses of trick or treating."

"But I was only nine at the time."

"This from a boy who called 911 to report a UFO."

"Other people saw it too."

"We're not getting off this train until we reach New York. Is that clear?"

A short while later, the train left Harrisburg and headed for Philadelphia. Marco tapped his foot nervously. His head ached from worry, and he wrung his hands, trying to release his pent-up nervousness that was growing by the second. He couldn't stand it. He paced back and forth in the aisle, feeling psychic vibrations of death and misery. In his mind, he began sensing the horror that he knew would descend upon his fellow passengers sometime soon. *Real soon.*

"Next stop, Philadelphia, the City of Brotherly Love!" boomed the conductor over the loudspeaker as the train pulled into the station and slowed to a stop. *This is it,* Marco thought. *The last chance. Do I stay with Abuelita? What if I'm wrong? What if there's not going to be an accident? What about those dreams? I don't want to die.*

"All aboard!"

What's the worst that can happen to me if I leave now? Abuelita has to — she just has to — follow me. She'll scream and yell, and Mom will ground me until high school gradua-

tion. *What's the worst that can happen to me if I stay on board? I could die!*

"Abuelita, I'm getting off!" Marco announced. Then he grabbed his suitcase and his grandmother's luggage off the overhead rack and marched to the door.

"Marco Luis! Get back here this instant!" she ordered.

"No!" With suitcases under both arms, he stood at the doorway. "Abuelita, come with me, please, please!" Then he scurried off the train and dropped the suitcases on the platform. His grandmother ran to the doorway in astonishment and anger. "Marco, what are you doing? What kind of stunt is this? Quit playing games. Hurry up and get back here."

"I'm not getting back on. You have to get off." The engine blew its whistle, and the train lurched forward and began to creep out of the station. "Abuelita! Get off! Now! Please!"

Swearing under her breath, his furious grandmother took a wary step. Marco reached out and yanked her safely to the platform. As the train slowly pulled out of the station, Marco looked up and saw Justin staring at him from the coach window. Justin had a look of doom in his eyes as he gave a halfhearted wave.

Now Marco had to face his ranting grandmother, who promptly gave him a furious tongue-lashing. "Are you happy now? Are you thrilled with this stunt of yours? Do you realize what you've done? You've ruined our trip. I am so angry at you. Wait till your mother finds out. I don't know what's gotten into your head, but when we get back home, you'd better see a psychiatrist."

Oh, brother, wondered Marco, *what have I done?*

"An untold number of people are reported dead this morning after a passenger train hurtled off an open drawbridge and into Newark Bay near Bayonne, New Jersey, last night."

The news from the TV that Abuelita had just turned on in their Philadelphia hotel room sent shock waves through the woman and her grandson.

"The span of the drawbridge had been opened to allow a freighter to pass underneath. For reasons that officials have yet to determine, the train sped past a warning signal to stop. The engine and three of the eight cars, including two passenger coaches, plunged into about forty feet of water. Early reports indicate that more than forty people are missing and presumed drowned. Rescue and salvage operations are underway searching for victims."

Abuelita dropped to her knees and wailed. She pounded the floor, screaming, sobbing, and praying.

Marco, who was still lying in bed, bolted up from the waist and then couldn't move. His arms and legs were paralyzed by shock. *This is a dream*, Marco thought. *Nothing but another bad dream.* His mind was too numb to comprehend all he was seeing and hearing on TV. His body shook with emotions — from sadness for the victims to relief that his dreams had saved his and his grandmother's lives. Then he broke down and cried.

"Now let's go to Dawn Farrell on the scene with one of the survivors." On the TV, a reporter stuck a microphone in front of a stunned, heavyset teenager who stood soaking-wet and barefoot. "What's your name?" asked the reporter.

"Justin Thomas."

Marco quickly wiped the tears from his eyes so he could better see his friend.

"Can you tell us what happened?" the reporter asked.

"I heard sounds of screeching metal. Then I got thrown out of my seat, and the train fell into the water. There were screams everywhere, and the coach started filling up with water. People were yelling, 'We're all going to die!' and things like that. My parents and I helped some of the passengers out the back emergency door. Then we had to jump into the oily water. We swam to the shore and climbed up a muddy bank. I swam back to the train and got tablecloths from the dining car, and we used those to wrap up our cuts."

Shaking his head in disbelief, Marco blurted out, "Everything I dreamed came true, Abuelita!"

By now, Abuelita had risen from the floor. Marco got out of bed, but his legs were weak and wobbly from all the emotion he felt. "How could I have doubted you, Marco?" she asked, tearfully hugging him. "You were right, you were so right. You and your dreams saved our lives!"

THE MAPLE TREE MURDERS

**T**he moment she walked by the maple tree, Jodi Armstrong felt the chill of death. She stopped in her tracks, clutched the arm of her boyfriend, and announced, "There was a murder here. A cold-blooded murder!"

"Not another one of your psychic visions," he moaned in disbelief.

"Call it what you want, but I feel that two people were murdered right here by this tree."

Jodi was about to become the last hope for the local police to crack a baffling mystery that had remained unsolved for more than twenty years.

* * *

The fifteen-year-old with the big brown eyes and long

85

black hair first displayed a psychic talent when she was ten. She discovered that when she concentrated on an object she held in her hand, she saw "little pictures in my mind like a speeded-up videotape." These visions revealed things about the object's owner.

At first, her family thought these visions were nothing more than an active imagination. But they began to believe in Jodi's psychic ability when they realized that almost everything she said turned out to be true. Once, Jodi wowed them when she held her Aunt Emily's ring in her hand and announced, "You have a secret that you haven't told anyone. Do you want me to tell?" When her aunt nodded, Jodi said, "You're going to have a baby!" Emily blushed and admitted to the family that she was pregnant. Then there was the time Jodi borrowed her older cousin Jeff's fountain pen and then told him, "You're planning to run away with Becky and get married without telling anyone, aren't you?" He admitted it was true, swore her to secrecy, and eloped a week later.

When Jodi entered high school in a small town in Missouri, she began practicing her psychic talent on her classmates. Jodi would hold an object such as a ring, bracelet, or letter sweater and answer questions such as, "Should I date Steve?" "Does Jenna like me?" "Will Shannon and I break up?" Jodi was the psychic "Dear Abby" of her high school.

Her reputation around town spread and soon adults were asking her questions about everything from finding lost pets to telling them what the future held. Although Jodi could have charged money, she never did. In fact, she did it as a service. "I'm afraid that if I make money off my gift, I'll lose my abilities," she once explained to her boyfriend, Ray Warren.

One Saturday, shortly after Ray received his driver's license, the two drove out to the country to enjoy a picnic lunch. The fall leaves were changing into dazzling shades of gold, red, yellow, and orange when they stopped at a hillside clearing.

"It's a picture-perfect day," said Ray. "The sun is shining, the leaves are turning ... and I'm with you."

"Oh, Ray, you're so sweet," said Jodi as she squeezed his hand. Pointing to the top of the grassy hill, she said, "That looks like a good place to have our picnic."

After walking for about 100 yards, they were passing by a lone, towering maple tree when Jodi stopped and gasped. In her mind, she saw several terrifying flashes: the face of a horror-stricken teenage boy ... the screams of a teenage girl ... the evil eyes of a madman ... the loud shots from a gun.

"What's the matter, Jodi?"

Jodi shuddered. "Oh, Ray, I see such awful things." Then she told him about her visions. "Those poor, poor kids," she said sadly. "They were murdered."

"Now hold on a second, Jodi. There haven't been any murders around here, or we would have heard about it. Besides, there's no sign of any shooting here."

"I get the feeling it happened a long time ago. Ray, your uncle is a police detective. Maybe he knows something about the murder."

"A *possible* murder," Ray said. "Maybe your imagination went bonkers from watching that *Nightmare on Elm Street* video Friday night."

"I predict you'll eat your words," she said.

"We'll see. But first, all I want to eat is lunch."

* * *

"As a matter of fact, Ray, there *was* a murder of two local teenagers. It happened back in the early 1970s. Let's see if I can find the file."

Ray gulped and slumped in his chair as his uncle, county sheriff's detective Richard Riley, dug around in the back of the bottom drawer of a metal file cabinet. "Here it is," Riley said, pulling out a tattered folder. "The only unsolved murder case in the department." Riley opened it up. "Sandra Dahlgren and her boyfriend Duane Peterson. She was sixteen, he was eighteen. It happened October 15, 1972. I was a deputy back then. A senseless, absolute tragedy. Both were shot, and their bodies dumped near Simmons Creek south of town. Never did find their car."

"Any suspects?"

"No. No witnesses, no murder weapon, nothing. We had very few clues. We talked to everyone we could think of and even asked for help from other law enforcement agencies. We came up with zip. There didn't seem to be any motive. They were good kids in the wrong place at the wrong time."

"Uh, Uncle Dick, this is going to sound really crazy, but I think my girlfriend Jodi Armstrong — you met her at Stan and Suzy's wedding — knows where they were shot."

Sitting behind his desk, Riley leaned forward, stared at his nephew, and asked, "And just how does she know that?"

"Look, I don't know how to explain this, but..." Then Ray told him about Jodi's terrifying visions by the maple tree. "Just talk to Jodi. Most people in town swear she's psychic ..."

"... and some say she's wacky."

"Uncle Dick, I've known Jodi since first grade, and we've been going steady for six months. I can tell you she's sweet and honest and sensitive. I don't understand all this psychic stuff — in fact, I kid her about it — but the truth is, she's usually right. What can it hurt to talk to her? Maybe somehow, some way, she can help. You have nothing to lose."

"Except maybe my badge," Riley grumbled.

* * *

"I have this overwhelming feeling of evil and death," said Jodi as she slowly walked around the maple tree. A short distance away stood Ray and Detective Riley, who was jotting down Jodi's words in a small notebook.

"The energy is really strong," she said. "I see a frightened girl, short blond hair, in a blue coat. She's leaning against this tree. And I see a tall, skinny boy with glasses, long hair, red jacket, with his back against the tree. They are both so, so scared."

Jodi gingerly touched the tree and then quickly withdrew her hand. "There's something inside this tree — some kind of evidence," she said. After a moment of concentration, she shouted, "Bullets! Yes, bullets!"

"How many?" asked Riley.

"Three ... no ... make that four." Then she slumped down to the ground and murmured, "I can't go on right now. It's too hard on me."

The next day, Riley used a metal detector, which revealed that four metal objects were embedded inside the tree trunk. He carved out a block of wood from the tree and, to his astonishment, discovered four bullets! The police lab confirmed that the bullets came from a .38 caliber pistol — the weapon police suspected was used in the murders. Further tests confirmed that the bullets had entered the tree more than twenty years ago. Using the metal detector, Riley then searched the area around the tree and uncovered an old, rusty .38 caliber pistol that had been buried about twenty yards from the tree.

"I confess I had my doubts," Riley told Sheriff Floyd Williams. "But everything Jodi Armstrong says is accurate. She described the victims and their clothes and how they were shot. Some of that information was not available to the press back then, so she couldn't possibly have known by reading old newspaper accounts. And the bullets. She found the bullets and that led us to the gun. The murderer probably killed the victims at the maple tree, buried the gun, dumped the bodies a couple of miles away at Simmons Creek, and took off out of town in their car."

"So what do you want to do next?" asked the sheriff.

"Police departments have used psychics to help on cases from time to time," said Riley. "I think this is one of those times when our department should do the same thing. Let me show Jodi some of the evidence. Maybe she can lead us to the killer."

"None of what she says can be used in a court of law," the sheriff reminded him.

"True, but she still might help us crack this case."

"Riley, we could get run out of town for this. However, when I retire next year, I want to leave knowing that this department solved every murder case while I was sheriff. Okay. Let's hear what Jodi has to say."

The next day, Jodi nervously sat down in a chair next to

Riley's desk. "Take your time," said Riley. "I'm going to show you some personal articles of the victims. See if you can pick up any psychic visions, okay?" Spread out on the desk were the bloodstained clothes worn by Sandra and Duane the day they were shot and other items of theirs.

Jodi closed her eyes, took a couple of deep breaths, and then slowly and deliberately touched the victims' items. She immediately received visions that flashed for a few seconds and then faded. She spoke haltingly and paused before seeing her next vision. "Sandra is very much in love with Duane ... they are sitting under the maple tree ... they hold hands and kiss. They talk about getting married, but they know they are much too young ... they talk and kiss some more ... they are so happy..."

Beads of sweat began to form on Jodi's forehead. She took some more deep breaths and continued.

"Duane likes to take Sandra to that maple tree. It's become their spot where they can talk about the future ... he feels so proud and happy to have Sandra as his girlfriend. He graduated high school and is waiting for her to do the same ... he loves cars and is a good mechanic, very handy ... he has dreams of owning a gas station and making enough money to marry her..."

Jodi began to shiver and her face twisted in fear. "I'm feeling something ... like they know they are being watched. Sandra thinks she saw a shadow in the bushes. They look. Suddenly, a scream! There's a man. He's creeping up on them and they see him. He's evil and he's got a gun. Sandra screams again. Duane tries to get up but the gunman orders him to freeze. Oh, they are so scared."

"Can you see what he looks like?" asked Riley.

"It's not too clear." She holds Duane's broken glasses in her hand. "This gunman is so mean-looking. His eyes are wild and crazy with eyebrows that point up. He's not as tall as Duane but he's a lot heavier. He has dark hair, all scraggly ... a round, scruffy face ... and a beard under his chin like the devil. He looks to be in his twenties. Duane wants to stay calm, but I feel in his heart he knows he's doomed. He tells Sandra not to panic but she keeps screaming. The man orders them to shut up."

"Do they know him?" asked the detective.

"No, they've never seen him before."

"Why is he doing this?"

"I don't know. He's making no sense at all, and they don't know what he's talking about. He calls them by some other names, something like Sharon and Bob. They tell him he's confused, that he's got the wrong people, and not to harm them..." Jodi broke down in tears. When she finally regained her composure she told Riley, "I don't know if I can go on. You know what happens next."

"Jodi, you're doing great," said the detective. "I know this is difficult for you, but please try. I'm going to hand you this pistol, and I want you to tell me anything you can about it."

Jodi shivered the moment she touched it. "It's the killer's," she said. "He's a desperate, crazy man. He just got out of prison. He's an angry man with a hair-trigger temper. He's in a big city ... near some kind of giant arch ... St. Louis maybe? He gets in an argument with some friends. He pulls out a gun — this one — and shoots one of them. The man looks dead. Another man and a woman who were with the victim take off, running in fear. The killer has to get out of town. He hops a freight train going west. He's filled with anxiety and tension. His mind is warped. He's afraid to go back to prison, afraid the two witnesses will squeal on him. He gets off the train near our town. He's crazed ... he's convinced the couple is after him ... he sees Sandra and Duane ... he calls them Sharon and Bob. Those must be the names of the witnesses. He says he has to get rid of them because they'll tell on him and he'll go back to prison ... Duane and Sandra plead for their lives, saying he's mistaken them for someone else. He gets angry and starts shooting until he runs out of bullets..." Jodi's face turned red, and tears rolled down her face. "I see nothing else."

"One more question, Jodi," said Detective Riley. "Do you know the name of the killer?"

Turning the weapon over and over in her hands, she said, "I can't make it out. Something with an 'M.'" She sighed. "Detective, this is too difficult ... I'm so tired..." Then she lay her head on the desk, too weak to move.

Jodi had never gone through such an emotional experience in her life. She was so exhausted that she went home, fell on her bed, and slept for nearly sixteen hours.

* * *

"Sheriff, you're not going to believe this," said Riley excitedly. "I just got off the phone with a buddy of mine at the St. Louis Police Department. I had him check all the murders that were committed there around October 15, 1972. He told me about one that happened the day before the Maple Tree Murders. A man by the name of Gary Phillips had been shot to death during an argument. The killer was a friend of Phillips — Mark Murray, a bad apple with an arrest record a mile long. They nabbed him a couple of years later in Memphis after an armed-robbery attempt. They brought him back to St. Louis and convicted him of second-degree murder. He's serving time at Missouri State Penitentiary."

"Is he our man?" asked Sheriff Williams.

"Could be. Jodi said she thought his name started with an 'M.' But it gets even better. There were two witnesses to Phillips' murder — Rob and Sherry Lawrence. Remember what Jodi said? She thought their names were Bob and Sharon. That's pretty darn close."

The sheriff whistled in disbelief.

"There's more. Take a look at this." Riley handed him Murray's mug shot. "The hair, the eyebrows, the beard — everything matches Jodi's description."

"Where do we go from here?"

"I think I'll go pay Mr. Murray a visit in prison and see what he has to say."

A few days later, when Detective Riley returned from the penitentiary, he had bad news for the sheriff. "Murray denied knowing anything about the Maple Tree Murders. Very uncooperative. Not only that but he's about to be set free because he's served his time. We don't have enough evidence to arrest him. There are no fingerprints on the gun and no witnesses to the crime other than Jodi's visions, which we can't use in court. He's going to get away with the murders unless we find something that can link him directly to the killings."

* * *

"Jodi," said Riley. "We need your help again."

"Oh, no," she said. "I don't think I'm up to it. That session just wiped me out. I still haven't recovered from it."

"Please, just one more time. Maybe there was some small detail that you didn't see the first time. Maybe there's some new clue you'll uncover. It's our only hope."

Reluctantly, Jodi agreed. The next day, holding the objects from the murder, she relived the killings committed by Mark Murray. Her account was almost identical to her first one, except for one new detail.

"After he kills them, Murray takes the money out of Sandra's purse and Duane's wallet. He rips the gold necklace and bracelet off Sandra. Then he spots Duane's ring. It's a big gold ring with the face of a knight in a helmet carved in a black stone. Murray yanks it off, admires it, and puts it on his own finger..."

* * *

Riley nervously paced back and forth outside the prison, knowing he had only one chance — a slim one — of nailing Mark Murray. Soon the gate opened up and Murray triumphantly walked out a free man.

"Well, well, well," said Murray with a snide smile. "If it isn't Detective Riley. Fancy meeting you here."

Riley's heart was pounding. He casually glanced at Murray's right hand, but not enough to tip off the ex-convict. What the detective saw made him even more anxious.

"Got a minute?" asked Riley.

"If it's about those murders, I already told you, I don't know anything about them," he snapped. "Now get lost."

"Oh, I think you know a great deal about those kids'

murders," said Riley. "In fact, I'm convinced you did it. But I have no proof." Extending his hand, he added, "So let me shake your hand for getting away with murder."

Cocking his head suspiciously, Murray stared menacingly into Riley's eyes. Then he broke out in a sinister grin and shook the detective's hand. Riley swiftly twisted Murray's hand just enough to see that he was wearing a ring with a black stone. The detective then gripped Murray's hand even tighter and took a closer look. Carved into the stone was the head of a helmeted knight! "Nice ring, Murray."

Murray's face turned white from shock. He had worn Duane's ring for so long that he had forgotten all about it. Murray instantly realized it was the one piece of physical evidence that could link him to the crime. He struggled to free his hand and growled, "I gotta go."

"You're not going anywhere — except back behind bars," Riley declared. "You're under arrest for the murders of Sandra Dahlgren and Duane Peterson."

AMY'S HUNCH

**A**my Drake had a hunch that her first trip to Mexico would be a memorable one. But nothing as terrifying as it turned out to be.

More often than not, whenever the pixie-faced, red-haired twelve-year-old had a hunch, she was dead-on right.

From the time she was five years old, Amy had displayed a sixth sense that astounded her family. She first demonstrated this ability on a trip to the mall with her father Sam, an extremely wealthy international businessman. As he reached into his back pocket to pay for a book he was buying for Amy, Mr. Drake let out a moan. "Oh, no, my billfold is gone!" He searched the bookstore and then checked the mall's lost-and-found department without success. "I bet I know what happened," he told his daughter. "A pickpocket took it."

"What's a pickpocket?" asked Amy.

"It's a good-for-nothing jerk who steals people's money from their pockets. Remember that guy who bumped into me on the way into the mall? He probably did that on purpose so he could swipe my billfold. I'd better report this to the mall police."

"I don't think he took it," said Amy.

"Why not?"

"I think you dropped it."

"Did you see it fall?"

"No. But maybe you should go back to the car and see if your billfold is there."

"If it fell out of my pocket, then somebody would have found it by now. Unless they're very honest, they won't turn it into the lost and found. But, okay, let's go see."

Mr. Drake thought his chances of ever seeing his wallet again were pretty slim. But as he reached his car, he looked down by the right front tire and spotted his billfold with all his money and credit cards still inside.

"It must have fallen out of my back pocket when I was getting out of the car," he told Amy. "This calls for a celebration — a double-scoop ice-cream cone with sprinkles because your hunch paid off, little lady."

"What's a hunch, Daddy?"

"It's like knowing something you didn't know you knew, but you felt like you knew anyway."

Amy didn't really understand her father's explanation, but she was thrilled that, because of her hunch — whatever that was — he had found his wallet.

A year later, another one of Amy's hunches proved to be a lifesaver. It happened when she threw a pretend tea party for her dolls under a big oak tree in the front of the family's mansion. With Amy's little "friends" seated in play chairs around a small table, her mother Linda sat on the grass next to her sipping tea, which was really cranberry juice. "Mommy, I think we should go inside."

"But we're not finished with our tea party, honey."

"Please, Mommy, now."

Her mother noticed that Amy kept staring at the clouds building up in the west. "Are you afraid of a storm?" she asked Amy. The girl nodded. "Don't worry," said Mrs. Drake. "I don't think it's going to rain for at least another hour or so."

Amy shook her head, grabbed her mother's hand, and pulled on it. "Mommy, we have to go inside! Hurry!"

No sooner had they reached the front door when a sudden bolt of lightning zigzagged down from the sky followed by a thunderous boom. Mrs. Drake wheeled around and, to her horror, saw that the bolt had struck the oak tree. With a loud cra-a-a-ack, a large thick branch snapped in two and crashed down, crushing Amy's little table.

Mrs. Drake's mouth dropped open in shock. "Honey, how did you know?"

Amy shrugged her shoulders. "I had a — what do you call it? Oh, yeah, a hunch."

Mrs. Drake reached down and hugged Amy as tightly as she could. She was afraid to say out loud what she was thinking. *We would have been killed if it hadn't been for Amy's hunch.*

There wasn't much doubt in the minds of Sam and Linda Drake that their only child possessed a special psychic gift — especially after what happened two years later.

Sam, who bought and sold real estate in several states and foreign countries, often invited business associates over to his mansion for dinner. Linda loved to cook fancy meals for guests with the help of their live-in housekeeper Maria. Together with Amy, they would set out the fine china, silver, and crystal on the dining room table. Amy, who was always included at these business dinners, was on her best behavior.

After one such dinner with two businessmen from Texas, Sam looked proudly at his green-eyed, freckle-faced daughter and said, "My guests told me you were just an angel tonight. A very pretty angel, I might add."

"Thanks, Daddy." But Amy wasn't smiling.

"What's the matter, darling?"

"Do you have to do business with those men?"

"Well, yes. We're about to close on a deal that could be worth almost a million dollars."

Amy, whose parents always encouraged her to speak her mind, declared, "I don't trust them. I think they're bad."

Sam kneeled down, looked Amy in the eyes and said, "Darling, I've already checked them out. They're respected businessmen. Why don't you trust them?"

"Just a hunch, Daddy."

"I can't cancel a million-dollar deal because you have a hunch."

"They acted nice at dinner, but they're bad," Amy insisted.

"What am I going to do with you?" said Mr. Drake, shaking his head and recalling how his daughter's hunches were usually right on the mark. After thinking for a moment, he said, "I'll tell you what. I'll have my staff run some further checks on them. It can't hurt."

Two weeks later, Sam came home with the biggest

stuffed panda bear Amy had ever seen. In fact, it was almost as big as her father. "This, my little angel, is for you."

"Oh, Daddy, I love it!" Amy said. "Thank you!"

"No, thank *you*. Remember when you said you had a hunch about those men who came over for dinner a couple of weeks ago? Well, my staff conducted another investigation and wouldn't you know, those guys turned out to be less than honest. They almost pulled off a scam that would have cost me nearly a million dollars."

* * *

When Amy turned twelve years old, her parents and Maria flew to Cancun, Mexico, a resort area on the Caribbean coast, for a vacation. "Mom, I have a hunch this is going to be a trip we'll never, ever forget," said Amy as she gazed out the window of the jetliner. "Something big is going to happen to us."

"Oh, I hope it's something good," said her mother.

"I do, too," added Amy. But already she was beginning to have a feeling that just the opposite might happen.

During the first few days of their trip, the family explored pyramids built centuries ago by the Mayan Indians. They snorkeled in the crystal-clear ocean teeming with the most brilliantly colored fish Amy had ever seen. In the afternoons, Maria, who was born and raised in Mexico, took Amy around to various outdoor markets so Amy could practice her Spanish.

Halfway into the vacation, Amy's parents left her with Maria while they flew to Mexico City. Mr. Drake had to attend several business meetings there. The Drakes were scheduled to catch a return flight a few days later on Thursday.

When Amy kissed her parents good-bye, she felt a slight uneasiness. But she didn't know why. After all, she was accustomed to having her parents travel regularly without her.

No matter where they were on their trips, the Drakes almost always called home every day to talk with Amy. But on Wednesday, the night before her parents were scheduled to return to Cancun from Mexico City, she hadn't heard from them.

"Maria, why didn't they call?" asked Amy as she got ready for bed.

"They probably tried, but couldn't get through," Maria replied. "Sometimes the telephones in Mexico don't always work. They'll be home tomorrow."

Amy tossed and turned in her bed before finally falling into a troubled sleep. Shortly before daybreak on Thursday, she awoke with a start and sat up in bed. Her heart pounded so hard she could almost hear the blood racing through her body. Suddenly, in her mind, she saw frightening images of a smashed-up plane ... toppled trees ... and the bloodied faces of her parents.

Amy let out a blood-curdling scream, jolting Maria from the other bedroom of their hotel suite.

"Amy! What's wrong?"

"I could see Mom and Daddy," she stammered, her eyes wide with terror. "They were in a plane crash in the forest, and they were hurt real bad. Oh, Maria, it was awful!"

"What a nightmare that must have been," said Maria,

clutching Amy's trembling body to her chest. "But that's all it was, a nightmare."

"No, Maria, this wasn't a dream. I was awake. Honest, I was. It was like a vision, a horrible vision. I could see the whole thing in my mind. I didn't dream it."

Maria knew better than to doubt Amy and her remarkable psychic abilities. "Maybe what you saw is a warning for them not to take that plane. Why don't I call them and suggest they try a different flight."

"It's too late," said Amy. "The plane crash isn't *going* to happen. It already *has* happened."

"But that's impossible. They're catching a flight later this afternoon."

"Maria, we've got to do something now. I'm telling you they've already crashed! They're lying there hurt. If we don't get them some help right now, they'll die!"

"Before we get crazy about this, let's see if they're still at the hotel, okay?"

Maria fumbled around the nightstand until she found the phone number of the hotel where the Drakes were staying in Mexico City. In her native Spanish, Maria asked the desk clerk if the Drakes had checked out of their room. With a sigh of relief, she turned to Amy and said, "See? They're still there. They haven't checked out." Back on the phone, she asked to be connected to the Drakes' room. It rang and rang but there was no answer. "I don't understand," she said to Amy while hanging up the phone. "They're both light sleepers. They would have answered if they were there. Maybe they had to get up real early this morning."

"At five in the morning?" Amy began to cry. "They're

in a plane crash and they're dying! We've got to help them!"

Maria called the airlines to find out if any planes were long overdue, but there were none. "What else can I do, Amy? The airlines say all their planes are accounted for."

Amy laid down on the bed, closed her eyes, and took several deep breaths to calm herself. Then she tried to summon another vision. "I see a cone-shaped mountain ... very steep sides ... a plane with no wings ... Mom and Daddy bleeding ... and the pilot is dead."

"Can you tell what airline it is?"

Amy concentrated hard before blurting out, "It's a small plane ... a private plane ... two engines."

Maria rushed to the telephone and called one of Mr. Drake's associates in Mexico City. Maria cried out in anguish when she learned that the Drakes had chartered a twin-engine plane early Wednesday morning. According to the flight plan, the Drakes flew to Veracruz about 250 miles from Mexico City to examine some land. Wednesday afternoon, they took off for the return trip to Mexico City. Not until Maria's call early Thursday morning did anyone realize the plane had not arrived and was missing.

Authorities immediately launched a search-and-rescue mission. Mexican military aircraft followed the flight plan of the doomed plane, but they failed to find a trace of the crash site in the mountainous region.

Throughout the morning, between bouts of sobbing, Amy continued to get visions of her severely injured parents. But the images remained the same, offering no new clue to the location of the crash site.

"If only I could tell where they are," said Amy. A moment later, she snapped her fingers. "Maria, you know that big map of Mexico they have hanging on the wall in the lobby? See if you can bring it up here."

Ten minutes later, Maria returned with a huge, rolled-up map that was as wide as the bed was long. "I had to bribe the desk clerk to let me borrow it," said Maria. "She thought I was nuts."

After shoving furniture aside, Amy spread the map out on the floor. She took a deep breath and slowly scanned every square inch of land between Veracruz and Mexico City. Then she closed her eyes and let her hands lightly glide over the map until she sensed a tingling in her fingertips. "I'm starting to feel something," she murmured. "I have a hunch they crashed right here." Her index finger pinpointed a spot about fifty miles west of Veracruz.

Maria leaned forward. "You've pointed to the north side of the volcano Citlaltepetl," she said excitedly.

"Call the searchers and get them to look over there!" Amy said.

Maria reached for the phone and then put it down. "No one is going to believe me if I say, 'This girl is psychic, and she says to search this area.'"

"Then let's tell a little fib. Tell them I talked to Mom and Daddy before they left Veracruz, and I just remembered that they said they were going to fly by the north side of the volcano to … um … photograph a waterfall."

The white lie worked. Even though the area wasn't near the planned flight path — the Drakes were supposed to fly ten miles south of the volcano — the search-and-rescue team combed the north side. Within an hour, Mexican

Army helicopters found the wreckage of a two-engine private plane — exactly where Amy had said it would be! And everything looked the same as she had described from her visions. The wings had been torn off from the impact of crashing into the side of the tree-covered volcano. The front of the plane was completely smashed and its fuselage, or body, looked like a crumbled tin can.

The area was too steep to land a helicopter, so medics were lowered to the spot of the crash where they found Linda and Sam Drake badly injured but alive. Linda Drake was bleeding from a head wound that caused her to slip in and out of consciousness, while Sam Drake had suffered two broken legs and several bad gashes on his arms and head. Tragically, the pilot had already died. The Drakes were treated at the crash site and then airlifted to a hospital in Mexico City.

Shortly before word reached Amy that her parents had been rescued, the anxiety and concern that had gripped her began to ease. Amy heaved a big sigh of relief and walked over to Maria, who was sitting on the floor, curled up like a ball, rocking back and forth in worry. "Maria, it's going to be all right. I have a good feeling that they've found Mom and Daddy alive."

Thirty minutes later the phone rang. Maria answered it and then relayed the information to Amy. "Great news!" she shouted. "Your parents..."

"...are alive!" Amy said, completing Maria's sentence. "I knew it! I just knew it!" Amy shouted joyously as she embraced Maria.

The following day, Amy, with Maria by her side, flew to the hospital in Mexico City to visit her parents in an emotional, tearful reunion. The Drakes told her that shortly after taking off from Veracruz, the plane tried to go around a thunderstorm. But a savage bolt of lightning struck the plane, knocking out all the navigation and communications equipment. Severe winds shoved the plane off course, and it plowed into the side of the volcano.

"No one knew you had crashed, except Amy," Maria told them. "She had a vision of the plane and that you were hurt. And she even knew where to find you!"

Sam Drake turned to Amy and gave her a wink. "Another one of your hunches, darling?"

"Yes, Daddy," said Amy, breaking out in a wide grin. "Just another one of my hunches."

THE MYSTERIOUS COLORS

Christopher Walker was six years old before he realized that none of his relatives or friends could see what he saw.

When he was a toddler, Chris just assumed that every person could see the pretty but faint rainbow colors glowing from their bodies. With the same concentration it took to spot an ant in the grass, Chris could observe a two-inch-thick "curtain" of light in various colors flowing ever so gently around each person.

The colors seemed brighter around a person's head, looking much like a faint halo. In Chris' eyes, people had some pretty neat colors slowly swirling around them, especially yellowy-gold, bluish-white, and orangish-red.

He didn't know that this strange and mysterious light is called an aura. He didn't know that only a few gifted psychic people in the world have claimed they can see auras. And he sure didn't know that his amazing ability would one day turn into a lifesaver.

* * *

To the sandy-haired, freckle-faced boy, some of the nicest people seemed to have an aura of a delicate rosy tint that turned into a soft purple.

"Grandma," Chris said one day when he was six years old, "I like your purple."

"But I'm not wearing anything purple, sweetheart," she replied. "My dress is red and white."

"I know that," said Chris. "It's your purple I like."

"What purple? Show me."

His little hand skimmed over the pale, wrinkled skin of her bare arms. Then he waved his hand over her head and smiled. "See the purple all over you? It's really pretty."

Grandma shook her head and chuckled. She had no idea what he was talking about.

"Do you like my colors?" Chris asked her.

Deciding to play along, Grandma answered, "Well, of course, I do. You have beautiful colors — bright red and green and..."

"No, I don't, Grandma." Holding out his arms, he said, "See, it's kind of white and kind of blue."

"Oh, yes, of course, now I see it." But even though he was only six years old, Chris could tell in her voice that Grandma couldn't *really* see his colors. So he entered the bedroom of his nine-year-old sister Ann Marie and asked, "Do you see my colors?"

"You're wearing a yellow shirt and red shorts," she replied.

"No, not my clothes, my *colors*," declared Chris, who was beginning to get frustrated. "You know, like..." he stopped for a moment to study her aura, "...like the orange that's around you."

Ann Marie gave him that "yeah, right" look and then stared in the mirror. "I don't know what you're talking about," she told him. "I don't see any colors around me or around you. You're crazy."

Chris stormed out of the room and went outside. He thought for sure that some of his friends could see the colors. Instead, the neighborhood kids laughed at him and told him he was making it all up. Now the youngster was totally confused. *I see the colors, so why can't anyone else?* he wondered.

When he returned home, he found his mother Betty had arrived from work. Chris gave her a kiss and hug and said, "Mom, Ann Marie says I'm crazy because she can't see my colors. And Nick and Dave and Jayne called me names and made fun of me because they said there's no such thing. And even Grandma couldn't see them."

"Slow down, honey. What colors?"

"The ones that kind of twinkle around you and me."

Betty Walker kneeled down so she was eye level with her son. "Sweetie, tell me exactly what you see."

He concentrated for a moment and said, "Well, you have bright blue that kind of sparkles around your head. And you have shiny white on your arms. Don't you see it?"

"No, sweetie, I don't." She could tell he was very disappointed by her answer. "But I believe that *you* can see the colors. So that makes you a very special person."

Chris brightened up. "Really? Oh, boy!" Then he took off running. "Hey, Ann Marie! Mom says I'm a very special person! So there!"

That night, as Chris was getting ready for bed, he overheard his parents talking with Grandma about him. "The best thing we can do," said his mother, "is just go along with him. He's got an active imagination. I'm sure he'll outgrow it over time."

"That's true," said his dad, Frank. "Remember, last year he had an imaginary dinosaur friend. What was his name? Oh, yeah, Freddy. Well, we haven't heard about Freddy for at least six months."

From that moment on, Chris decided not to say anything more about the colors he was seeing. He would just keep it all to himself. Over the next few years, his ability to see the auras of other people — especially strangers — seemed to fade a bit as he grew older. He had to concentrate harder than ever to detect their auras. It was much easier for him to see the auras of people whom he knew well.

Eventually, by the age of ten, Chris discovered a link between the color of the aura and a health problem. Although the colors of a person's aura seemed to "bleed" from one shade to another, such as orange into yellow, occasionally Chris would detect a lone color different than the rest of the auras. This color — usually a faded red with a dark edge and shaped like an egg — would hover over a certain part of the body at the point where the person was ill.

Chris first tested his theory one day when his dad came

home from the office. After noticing a red splotch in the aura around his father's head, the boy asked, "Dad, are you feeling okay?"

"So-so."

"Um, do you have a headache?"

"Actually, I do. How did you know?"

"Just a guess."

A few days later, while watching TV with his grand-mother, Chris turned to ask her a question when his eyes caught sight of a red spot bordered in black in the aura around her left elbow. "Grandma, is your elbow hurting you?" he asked.

When it came to her health, Grandma seldom would admit that anything was wrong. "That's a strange question to ask me," she said. "There's nothing wrong with my elbow. Why do you ask?"

"I was just wondering." Right when he thought he had it all figured out, Chris was wrong. Or was he?

Later that evening, Grandma was tidying up the kitchen alone and didn't see Chris walk in. She grimaced in pain and rubbed her elbow. Then she reached into her pocket and took out some pills. Only after she swallowed them did she notice Chris.

"Your elbow *is* hurting you, isn't it?" Chris said.

"It's nothing really," Grandma replied. "Just some arthritis — one of the 'joys' of growing old. How about some ice cream?" As she fixed him a bowl, she said, "You asked me about my elbow this afternoon. How did you know it was hurting?"

"I saw the color ... um ..." He didn't want Grandma or anyone else to think he was still seeing auras. So he told a little white lie. "I saw you rubbing it, and it looked like you were hurting."

"That's strange. I've made a point of not touching it in front of anyone. Now listen. This arthritis is nothing, so don't go telling anyone about it, okay?"

"I promise, Grandma."

In school, Chris began studying the auras of his close friends. He could tell if they were suffering from a cold, headache, stomachache, sore throat, or fever. He could also detect which kids were faking illness when they asked to be excused from class to visit the school nurse. He didn't know what to do with this strange ability to "see" health problems, so he chose not to do anything about it.

One day while visiting Hudson's Department Store, where his mother sold furniture, Chris was joking around with Dotty Beamon, his mother's good friend and fellow salesperson. Mrs. Beamon was an older, gray-haired woman who had a smile as big as her wide waist.

"Congratulations, Chris," she boomed loud enough for everyone in the furniture department to hear. "I heard you won the school's spelling bee. Let's see you spell smarty-pants — backwards."

"S-T-N-A-P-Y..." Chris stopped in the middle of his spelling when he noticed a dark red aura shimmering right over Mrs. Beamon's heart. He wondered, *Maybe I should say something. But what could I tell her? "Gee, Mrs. Beamon, you've got a strange-looking aura around your heart. Maybe you should have it checked out." Better keep quiet.* "...T-R-A-M-S."

Two days later, his mother Betty came home late from the store in tears.

"Mom! What's wrong?" asked Chris with alarm.

"It's Dotty. She had a heart attack. She was talking to a customer when she collapsed. It was awful. I gave her CPR, and the paramedics came right away and rushed her to the hospital. It's such a shock. Why, I don't think she had missed a day of work in ten years."

Chris didn't hear much of what his mother said after she had uttered the words "heart attack." The news had triggered a wave of guilt that bowled him over. *If only I had told Mrs. Beamon,* he thought. *If only I had explained what I saw, maybe she would have gotten help in time.*

"Is she going to be all right?" Chris asked.

"The doctors don't know for sure, honey. But they think so."

From that day on, Chris began paying closer attention than ever before to the auras of his loved ones. He didn't want anything bad to happen to them.

A few weeks later, as the family hustled to get ready in the morning, Chris was eating his cereal when a sight jolted him so much that he dropped his spoon. In the lower right side of his mother's chest, Chris noticed a very faint color in her aura he that he'd never seen before. It was a red spot about the size of a dime.

"Are you feeling all right, Mom?"

"I'm fine, how are you?"

"Uh, fine. Well, I have to go. I love you."

At school, Chris went to the library and looked up a picture of the anatomy of the human body. He wanted to find out what part of his mother's body was ailing. Unfortunately, he couldn't tell from the book. It was either a problem with her stomach muscle, large intestine, liver, or lung.

Chris prayed that the red spot would disappear, but it grew slightly larger with each passing day. His mother seemed in good health. Even though she was a little tired and had a slight cough, she otherwise felt fit. Still, Chris fretted. He had to say something before it was too late.

"Mom, will you do something for me?" he asked.

"If I can, honey, what is it?"

"Would you go see a doctor?"

"A doctor? What for?"

"I think there's something really wrong with you. It's somewhere in your chest."

"Well, Dr. Walker, just how do you know that?"

Chris didn't want to tell his mother about the red spot in her aura. "I can tell."

"Oh, really?" she said, her eyebrows rising. "And how can you tell? Did you graduate from medical school when I wasn't looking? Or perhaps you took a correspondence course at the Swami School of Fortunetellers."

"Come on, Mom, I'm serious. Just go to the doctor for a checkup, okay? Would you do that for me?"

After a moment's thought, Betty agreed. "Well, I haven't had a physical in a few years, and after what happened to Dotty, maybe it's time. All right, if it'll make you happy, I'll go. But I'm telling you, there's nothing wrong with me — nothing a nice vacation wouldn't cure."

On the day of his mother's appointment with the doctor, Chris ran all the way home from school to find out what was wrong with his mother. "Well?" he asked her. His heart sank at first when she grimly shook her head.

Then, noticing the look of worry on her son's face, Betty hugged Chris and said, "Oh, that was mean of me to do that to you." Breaking out in a big grin, she announced, "I'll have you know that the doctor says I'm in excellent health for a woman my age who's a mother, wife, and full-time saleslady. How about that? Now you don't have to worry about me anymore."

"That's great, Mom!" Chris felt so relieved — for a short while. But that red spot in her aura was not going away. In fact, it continued to grow to twice the size of a quarter, and the edges were becoming darker.

"Mom, did the doctor say anything about your lungs or your liver or your intestines?" Chris asked.

"No, why?"

"There's still something wrong with you."

"Young man" — his mother never called him that unless she was angry — "you've got to stop this right now! I went to the doctor at your insistence, and I'm fine. Now stop this nonsense."

Chris took a deep breath. Convinced it was a matter of life or death, he had no choice but to tell her the truth and hope she'd believe him. "Mom, listen to me. I don't know how or why, but I can see things other people can't. Remember when I was a little kid and I told you I could see colors glowing around people? Everyone laughed it off as my imagination. So I shut up about it. But I've always been able to see them. I've just never said anything about it. I found out in a book that these colors are called auras. Now I can tell by looking at an aura where someone is sick or hurting. I can see my friends' sore throats and Dad's headaches."

Betty Walker's mouth dropped open in shock. Rather than write off what her son was saying as the silly ravings of a grade schooler, she believed Chris because she had never known him to lie.

"Mom, I saw Mrs. Beamon's aura. It was different around her heart a couple of days before she had her heart attack. I saw Grandma's arthritis in her elbow before anyone ever knew about it. I've been watching your aura. And you've got a dark red spot."

"Where, honey?"

Chris gently poked his finger under her right rib. "There's something bad there, Mom. I can see it. You've got to get it checked out."

"You're pointing at my lung. But I don't feel any pain or discomfort there. And I can breathe fine."

"You've got to get an X-ray or something, please," Chris pleaded.

"Okay, honey, okay."

Betty made an appointment with a lung specialist for the following week. When the day arrived, she almost canceled because she thought it would be a waste of time and money. But, knowing how concerned Chris was, she went ahead and had a chest X-ray.

Amazingly, Chris was right. X-rays showed a spot on the lower part of her right lung and further tests revealed that it was cancer. Betty was whisked immediately into the operating room where the surgeon removed the cancerous tumor.

"You were very lucky," the doctor told Betty after she was wheeled into the recovery room. With her husband, son, and daughter standing by her bed, Betty breathed a sigh of relief. "We caught the cancer in the nick of time," said the doctor. "It looks like you're going to make a full recovery."

Tears of happiness began streaming down Chris' face. "Had the cancer gone untreated for too much longer," the doctor added, "it probably would have been too late."

"Thank you, doctor," Betty said. Then she grabbed Chris' hand, squeezed it tightly, and said, "Thank you, sweetheart — for saving my life."